MW01282500

The Making of a Statesman

By Narada Muni, the Guru of all Statesmen

"Dedicated to all political leaders of the world."

ADITYA SATSANGI

A Must Read Book

"Narada Muni has often been misrepresented by mischievous writers and media. Oftentimes, he has been depicted as a comic personality in publications, TV and media. With this book for Statesmen, the author presents Narada as the Guru of all Statesmen. This book is a bonafide translation from a brief conversation between Yudhishthira and Narada as mentioned in Mahabharata of Vyasadeva. The reader will enjoy the depth of summary instructions given by Narada to Yudhishthir on Governance and Statecraft.

Through Yudhishthira, Narada Muni is actually instructing all statesmen of this world. These instructions are valid today more than ever and will remain so for the remainder of eternity. This book will serve as a guiding light to many in active politics. Narada Muni is not only a great traveling Saint but also the Foremost Thinker, Social Reformer, Economist and a Spiritual Scientist who knows the science of God. Political Leaders will gain trust and love of their people by using these instructions. A must read for every Politician who aspires to become a Statesman."

Disclaimer

This book falls into the category of non-fiction. The book contains historical information from Mahabharat as well as the author's study of political events. The book is a commentary from a centrist or Dharmic perspective and is particularly designed to make the reader think about the condition of politics today. Sattology is a copyright by the author in the USA. The author is a scholar in Vedic scriptures and as such he has quoted scriptures as deemed necessary to increase the faith of millions of Dharmic people. The commentary on International Historic events is based on the author's viewpoint. Political lessons from Anushasana Parva of Mahabharat and Chanakya's Arthashastra are also covered in some parts in italics.

"History is what it is and it is Sattology, anything else Mythology. Any History of the world that doesn't trace its connection with Mahabharata (compiled by Vyasadeva and written by Ganesh) is a Mythology.

Narada, the Guru of all LokPals

"A must read for all Politicians who aspire to become Statesmen."

About Aditya Satsangi, the author

"He has been a lifelong practicing Hindu with a Bhakti Shastri title in Brahma Madhva Sampradaya. With his inherent love for Vedic literature, he presents the most authentic account of Narada Muni's instructions to Yudhishthira on how to become a successful Statesman. In his first successful book, Sattology - Debunking Mythology, Aditya Satsangi invented a new term Sattology which is a true antonym of Mythology. Readers will find his writings to be deeply engaging and interesting. Aditya has mastered the art of Narration and his second book not only engages but also educates the reader."

Copyright Aditya Satsangi 2019
First published in 2019 by Sattology Everyday Chat Inc.

ISBN: 9798357849519
India: INR 750 / USA: $29.99

"The moral rights of the author have been asserted.
All rights reserved. No part of this book may be reproduced, or stored in a retrieval system, or transmitted in any form or by any means, electronic, mechanical, photocopying, recording, or otherwise, without express written permission of the publisher and without the approval from the author. The views expressed in this work are solely those of the author and do not necessarily reflect the views of the publisher, and the publisher hereby disclaims any responsibility for them."

Published by:

Sattology Everyday Chant Inc. (a non-Profit registered in California, USA)
San Diego, USA 91902
sattology@sattology.org

www.sattology.com

Dedicated To

My Guru
Protectors of Sanatana Dharma
My Children
And above all to Brahma Madhva Sampradaya

Content

Foreword

"In common with other great contemporaneous civilisations, such as the Roman, the Greek, the Egyptian and the Chinese, the mother lode of the six millennia of Indic civilisation contains much that remains relevant in the modern age. Slowly, painfully, this heritage is being excavated from the crevices in which much of it had been hidden by the nine centuries of servitude that the people of India faced, a situation that ended - legally, at least, in 1947. Ancient texts and sayings are being discovered, while the time may come when Ayodhya,Kashi and Mathura (which are as important to Hindus as Mecca and Medina are to the Muslim faith) reclaim their traditional character. Rather than government, it is individuals across the world that are responsible for such a revival of not simply attention but knowledge of the hitherto lost millennial layers of the history of India. Among the most diligent of such individuals is Aditya Satsangi, who has worked for over a decade in the task of showing why those who spring from the Indic heritage can be proud of that fact, and seek to uphold the values that nearly a millennium of servitude almost caused to be lost forever. Thank you, Aditya"

- **Professor Madhav Das Nalapat (UNESCO Peace Chair | Manipal University, INDIA)**

'Worth Reading …..'

- **Dr Subramanian Swamy**

"Narada Muni says - Whether you consider humans to be an eternal Jivatma (living being) or a temporary body, or even if you accept an indescribable opinion that he is both eternal and temporary, you do not have to lament in any way. There is no cause for lamentation other than the affection which has arisen out of delusion. (1.13.44)"

The tradition of statecraft existed for centuries without any major influence from orthodox Brāhmaical theology, but that sometime in the early centuries of the Common Era this changed. The Artashastra vividly captures this shift. The transformation of Indian Sub-continent political thought is then mapped briefly in other areas and placed in the context of the "Brahmanical revival" of the second-fourth centuries CE and the onset of the "Sanskrit Cosmopolis" in the third century CE.

The question of whether a pre-modern Indian author, Kautilya, who addressed statecraft and intelligence in a scholarly fashion, might bear a meaning for contemporary Intelligence Studies. Kautilya and Chandragupta Maurya, a near-contemporary of Aristotle and Alexander, viewed intelligence as a central feature of statecraft. While not yet employing the category 'intelligence', the concept of intelligence is very much present in Kautilya's opus magnum Arthashastra, which can be translated as 'Textbook of Statecraft and Political Economy'.

Kautilya provides a detailed account of intelligence collection, processing, consumption, and covert operations, as indispensable means for maintaining and expanding the security and power of the state. His understanding of intelligence analysis is outstanding.

Aditya, in his book has taken Narad muni's view which came before Kautilya's, and might have inspired him as well, as a platform for understanding a complex and very interesting topic of statecraft. In today's world when so much depends on the political decisions, be it eradication of poverty, diseases, global warming, financial stability, human development parameters or nuclear button click, this knowledge will help the political fraternity to handle such scenarios in more righteous way, that is also called the Dharma way of decision making!

I wish Aditya Satsangi my best wishes and hope this book makes it to the bestseller category soon. I will request more people to read this book.

"Aum Asato mā sad gamaya, Tamaso mā jyotir gamaya
Mṛtyormā amṛtam gamaya, Aum śānti śānti śāntiḥ "

- **Sharad Mohan**

-   *Author of Bestseller "Kashmir – The Bermuda Triangle of India" and India –An Unbroken Civilization.*

About Sattology:

Bharat[48] is a land where many faiths have originated or inspired by Vedic teachings. Vedic means based on Vedas and Vedas mean knowledge. Every part of Vedic knowledge is taken as an axiomatic truth and can be subjected to scientific scrutiny and scientific research. All of them have come to be scientifically validated. Histories mentioned in Mahabharata and Ramayana which are also connected to Vedas have also been corroborated through scientific, archeological, and historical research. Thus, they are not considered mythology also, rather I call them 'Sattology'. Mythology means a study of lies or imaginary history, Sattology means a study of truth or true history. Myth means Imaginary, Sat means factual. I invented this term to challenge western academicians and historians.

Acknowledgement

नारायणं नमस्कृत्य नरं चैव नरोत्तमम् ।

देवीं सरस्वतीं व्यासं ततो जयमुदीरयेत् ।।

I offer my humble obeisances to Shri Nara and Narayan , Mother Saraswati , Vyasadeva before I read historical texts collectively known as Jai (जय).

My acknowledgement to all historians who have endured prosecution at the hands of powerful & tyrants alike for bringing forth truth.

My acknowledgement to all who have endured persecution to fight corruption. Books and lectures of Srila Prabhupada inspired significantly to bring forth this historical rendering.

Seeking shelter and blessings of Ganesha, the original transcendental scribe.

My humble obeisances to all great Gurus in the Brahma Madhva Sampradaya, Adi Shankaracharya and also Sri Sampradaya who inspired me to read Mahabharat and Ramayan. My unlimited thanks and gratitude to my children Vaidehi and Govind who allowed me to concentrate on my research and writing. *This book will guide all statesmen for all time to come.*

The Setting

Maharaja Yudhishthir, the emperor of the world was given half of the kingdom by his father's elder brother after much philosophical persuasion and political pressure including threat of self-defeating war.

Yudhishthir and his capable brothers and their Mother, Kunti, survived multiple assassination attempts on their lives during the course of their lives with the blessings of Vasudeva and other well-wishers like Vidura. There were always assassination attempts on them by different agents sent to them by their evil cousin Duryodhan.

Duryodhan's father, Dhritarashtra was a noble man blinded by his eldest Son's ambitions. Pandavas father Pandu was the younger brother of Dhritarashtra. Dhritarashtra was blind and therefore his younger brother Pandu was made the king.

Dhritarashtra had no enviousness towards his younger brother because he accepted his fate as the work of destiny. He even advised his son Duryodhana initially to give up their hatred towards Pandavas.

Duryodhana suffered from inferiority complex vis-a-vis pandavas. Pandavas were all qualified beyond any human estimations on all areas of human index. They were rich, beautiful, chivalrous, skilled, successful and humble.

Their personal qualities made them dear to everyone including Krishna. That generated lots of envy in their enemies such as Duryodhana. Duryodhana had already usurped their kingdom by guile but when they staked their claim, he carefully avoided until he was forced to part his kingdom.

His father Dhritarashtra gave a barren land to Yudhishthir. When Yudhishthir saw the land, he wondered what he could do with that land. But he quietly accepted that land as the will of providence. That was his biggest qualification.

Introducing Yudhishthira

Yudhishthir Maharaja was a noble soul that even enemies wouldn't stop appreciating his qualities. His complexion was fair, body thin, tall with sharp facial features and a very humble personality.

He was the master of diplomatic conversation and a master economist. His knowledge of ArthaShastra was extremely well known that even Narada Muni who is considered topmost artha shastri acknowledged it and didn't instruct him in that subject.

In those times all Kings were expected to understand ArthaShastra[34] because it involves a very detailed study of Varnashrama. ArthaShastra without Varnashrama doesn't make sense. Yudhishthir, being the qualified prince, had mastered Artha Shastra along with all of his 4 brothers.

Introducing Bhim

Bhim , the second in command after Yudhishthir, was as qualified as Yudhishthir in all qualities.

In addition he had unparalleled bodily strength being the son of Vayu. He could perform tasks that were difficult for the strongest human bodies.

Introducing Arjun

His younger brother was Arjun, the best warrior in the world and the chief of the Army of Maharaja Yudhishthir. He had access to all types of weapons and knowledge.

He was a tall man, very muscular arms, long arms full of strength, fair skinned and always ready to carry out war on orders of his elder brother and mother.

He was humility personified and gentle to everyone. He never raised his voice on his teachers, brothers, society and anyone who came to his shelter willingly or unwillingly. But to his enemies, he was death personified.

Introducing Nakul and Sahadeva

Arjun's younger brothers were twins - Nakul and Sahadev. Being the sons of Celestial Ashwini Kumaras, both were tall, very fair skinned, very muscular, expert in all military warfare skills and never lost any war just like their elder brothers. In addition they were the best Artha Shastri. They were the best looking of all the five brothers.

Between, Nakul and Sahadeva, Nakul was the best looking of all five brothers so much so that when Pandavas were leaving for exile, he was asked by Yudhishthira to cover his body with mud so that women don't obstruct them to even come out of the palace.

Sahadeva was the darling of Yudhishthira and Kunti Maharani. Sahadeva was also an expert on Vedic shastra and would regularly give spiritual discourses on Bhakti and devotional practices.

Sahadeva being the youngest of all Pandava was a darling of all his elder brothers and his mother Kunti.

These five brothers were the darling of the entire population. They attracted everyone around them by virtue of their good qualities. Their teachers were fond of them, Krishna loved them, women & children loved them and their opponents feared them.

The higher beings from heavenly kingdoms showered their blessings on them. These five brothers underwent significant hardships after the demise of their father. But they never complained nor ever found faults with anyone else for their misfortune.

They were always grateful. Their attitude attracted sages, devatas and many other divine personalities. They conquered heavenly kingdoms, got weapons from higher beings, had all riches in their command but they were never attached and remained always humble.

They surrendered their lives to the will of Krishna and therefore they were always victorious. At the same time they never relinquished their duties to anyone else. For them their kartavya was everything. A man becomes great by their actions. Pandavas were great because their actions were in accordance with Vedic Shastra.

When pandavas were again discovered after lakshagraha (assassination attempt on their lives by burning the house they were invited to live in along with their mother) and their marriage to Draupadi , they were invited to the capital by Dhritarashtra (after good counsel by his secretaries and sages).

Vidura arranged for a boat with yantra or motor to ferry Pandavas and Kunti through river Ganga to a safe location. This is a fact. Vedic Bharat was the first inventor of motorized transport and it's a fact. Western claims of technology superiority is a recent phenomenon after World War II.

They were offered half of the kingdom of Hastinapur and were given a barren piece of land called Khandav Van. With their hard work and perseverance they built a fabulous kingdom in that barren land. They started managing their kingdom in accordance with the knowledge that they had received.

They quickly achieved the desired success. Their kingdom was powerful, rich and the people that they were taking care of were extremely pleased by their rule. Their kingdom attracted all the wealth, intelligent people and divine personalities.

Then came Narada Muni, the foremost of thinkers, to their kingdom. He wanted to check on King Yudhishthir, whether he was ruling as per the code of conduct for the kings. It is the duty of teachers to check on their pupils and that's exactly what Narada Muni is doing here.

This is where my book begins. The questions that Narada asks Yudhishthir while checking on him will guide many kings or Heads of State or Prime Minister or Presidents to come in future generations. For the purpose of simplicity, I will use the term Lokpal for Head of State. So whenever you see a term LokPal which means maintainer of People, I am actually referring to the Head of State.

As a service to all humanity, I will be elaborating on these questions keeping in view the spirit of the original author Vyasadeva and the original scribe Ganesh. This is my humble attempt to serve them. The king in this book may also allude to democratically elected heads of state in today's times or LokPal.

The quality of politics defines the well being of citizens. For the purpose of this book, I won't compare the current political philosophies in detail but I am going to summarize a few points.

Political Philosophies Today

Four broad Political Philosophies and their principal ideologies today:

- Socialism : Class less society
- Capitalism: Profit only mindset
- Communism: Production only Mindset
- Dharmic economy: Values based mindset.

The concept of Left wing and Right wing grouping has a French origin in that the Left is opposed to the administration and the Right is pro administration. The bicameral seating arrangement in the French Parliament defined these groups. The Hindu or Vedic way takes a middle path focussed on Dharma. Dharma is also the most logical and truth oriented path. *Democracy is failing in the USA as well as most European nations because it was designed to take away the rights of minorities. Democracy is also an easy method of intervention by the west in other countries through managed political disturbances. The west is rich because they have exported their democratic models to other nations which allows them an easy leverage to demand favorable business deals.*

Often times, we hear the new political terms such as #GreenNewDeal, Leftist Conservatives, Left-wing (Pan-African, Pan-Latin American, Pan-Islamic Leftists, Gender based, White Nationalism, Pan-Arabism, Pan-Islamic liberals) and Classical Liberalism used extensively by politicians.

Leftist conservatives in the political system haven't defined themselves well enough. Leftist conservatives are almost an extinct species in many ways. Leftist conservatism goes hand in hand with most civilized societies today. Leftist conservatism can also be called the new centrist. But it is still not the best compared to Dharma.

Liberal or Left-Wing politics promotes egalitarianism and social equality in complete disregard to existing social hierarchy. Classless society is a utopian idea that cannot be implemented. The race politics in today's political landscape is classical left-wing political philosophy. Herein, the left parties have used racial tones to become a champion of racial equality. Historically, Left were the supremacists and Right were the people in power.

Oftentimes, nationalism is derided by left-wing politicians. Nationalism is also derided by left-wing Pan-Islamic politicians because of their wahabi Islamic connections. African Socialism, Latin American Socialism, Third worldism, pan-Islamism or Islamic-Communism are classical thought processes of left wing politics in the world today. Most of those philosophies have produced anarchy in civil societies because these philosophies are against Dharma.

None of the prevalent political philosophies can help maintain peace in today's human society because they are against Dharma. Dharma is a natural platform for truth & justice. Without Dharma, there will always be differences between nations and also a general unrest amongst people in all countries of the world. If we carefully analyze the world map then we will observe that the entire world appears to be one unified land surrounded by oceans. *The only disconnect in continuous land appears to be the fifty mile separation known as the*

Bering Strait between Alaska and Russia. As per geologists, this shallow strait is just 300 ft in depth. According to geologists, this was a continuous land through which people from Asia migrated to the Americas. That's why the DNA of most natives of America carries a strand from Asia as per geologists.

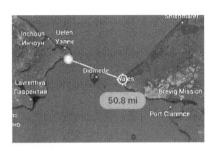

50 Miles separation between Asia and Americas

The continents of Africa and Asia are also interconnected through Land. *The Suez Canal is a man-made transit for ships.*

The continents of North America and South America are also connected through land. *The Panama Canal is a man-made transit for ships.*

Most armies of Sugreev used land routes as well as sea routes to search for mother Sita all over the world. *Maharaja Yudhishthir also used land routes to conquer the whole world for Sanatana Dharma.* Sea routes were used by European Colonizers to enslave all continents for 'Gold, Glory and God' for their vatican church. *Please read my book by the same title available on Amazon.* Soviet Communism, American Democracy, European Socialism and Chinese Communistic Capitalism have all failed to bring happiness to their citizens. Gradually, people are becoming dissatisfied with all the current political ideologies because those ideologies have exploited everyone. *Generally, people are not happy with any of the current political systems because all of them focus on exploitation.*

Dharma is a centrist philosophical model which is neither left, nor right. Dharma becomes the philosophical model when it is practiced in conjunction with Varnashram and Arthashastra. Varnashrama is a natural order of any society. Varna means categories which are broadly recognized as Brahmana (teachers), Kshattriya (protectors), Vaishya (business persons) and Shudra (workers). *These categories grouped around professions exist in every society naturally. The skills needed for each of these occupational categories are mutually exclusive.* Ashrama means social order. It is based on the age of people. Students (up to 25 years of age), Married Couples (up to 50 years of age), Travelling Married Couples (up to 75 years of age) and exclusive spiritual pursuit (after 75 years of age). *When occupational categories are combined with social order then an ideal happy society emerges. The purpose of this social system is spiritual advancement of the general populace. When governments focus on this, then they actually focus on the real development of people that they govern.* Loktantra is the political governance system that exclusively focuses on implementing Varnashrama, thereby ensuring happiness, longevity and wealth to everyone without any discrimination.

The Sattology of Characters

Krishna or Vasudev: Bhagavan, Source of all, Master of all. A loving personality that cares about everyone

Narada: Tall, Fair, Intelligent and very educated personality that cares about everyone in the world. A deeply knowledgeable person and a super excellent teacher of all. He is a master in all departments of knowledge such as Economy, Warfare, Arthashastra, music, science of elements, and much more

Yudhishthir: Eldest Son of Pandu. Tall, thinly built, fair skinned, Gentle natured, Expert Artha Shastri, Master of all Vedic Shastra and heir to the kingdom of his father, Maharaja Pandu. The Emperor.

Bhim: Younger Brother of Yudhishthir. Tall, very strongly built, dark complexioned, always respectful and second in command to Maharaj Yudhishthir. Conquered Eastern provinces up till Cambodia for Maharaj Yudhishthir's Rajasuya Sacrifice

Arjun: Younger brother of Bhim. Fair complexioned, expert archer, best warrior, humility personified and a close friend of Krishna. Conquered northern provinces up till Arctic Ocean for Maharaj Yudhishthir's Rajasuya Sacrifice

Nakul: One of the Twin younger brothers of Arjun. Extremely good looking, expert warrior, very gentle. Conquered western provinces up till Mediterranean Sea for Maharaj Yudhishthir's Rajasuya Sacrifice

Sahadev: Twin brother of Nakul. Extremely good looking, expert warrior, very gentle. Conquered southern provinces up till Sri Lanka for Maharaj Yudhishthir's Rajasuya Sacrifice

Dhritarashtra: Eldest brother of Maharaja Pandu. Blind by birth. Excellent Knowledge of Vedic Shastra. Expert and righteous King

Pandu: Younger Brother of Dhritarashtra

Duryodhan: Son of Dhritarashtra. Great knowledge of Shastra. Expert in managing the Kingdom. Great Warrior. Envious of his Cousin brothers, sons of Pandu.

Mahabharat: The epic prose written by Ganesh, the original scribe ; compiled by Vyasadeva, the original author ; under the directions and blessings of Brahma (the Supremely divine person born from the navel of Vishnu). It is also defined as the history of the Kings of the Bharat dynasty. It also means instructions with deep meaning for humanity.

Vyasadeva : Son of Parashar and Satyavati who divided the original Vedas into four

Pandava: Sons of Pandu (Yudhishthir, Bhim, Arjun, Nakul, Sahadev)

LokPal: the Head of State, President, Prime Minister, Supreme Leader of People & State

Bhupal: the local or regional head of a piece of land under LokPal

Who is Narada?

Narada Muni's birth and activities form the basis of all Puranic activities as we know today. He has been a principal source of information being shared across the multiple lokas (लोक - places of residences of multiple types of living beings).

Narada, the Guru of Dhruv

Dhruv was the son of Uttanapada and Suniti. In order to get a Kingdom greater than his Grandfather Brahma, he wanted to go to the forest to perform austerities. His mother Suniti directed him to worship Hari[1] him to remove his distress and get what he wanted. Thereafter, with determination and intelligence he left for the forest to search for Hari. The great sage Nārada overheard this news, and understanding all the activities of Dhruva, he was struck with wonder. He approached Dhruva, and touching the boy's head with his all-virtuous hand, he spoke as follows. *Narada Muni observed, 'How wonderful are the powerful kṣatriyas (warriors) ! They cannot tolerate even a slight insult to their prestige. Just imagine! This boy is only a small child, yet harsh words from his stepmother proved unbearable to him.'*

The great sage Nārada told Dhruva:

1. My dear boy, you are only a little boy whose attachment is to sports and other frivolities. Why are you so affected by words insulting your honor?
2. My dear Dhruva, if you feel that your sense of honor has been insulted, you still have no cause for dissatisfaction.

This kind of dissatisfaction is another feature of the illusory energy; every living entity is controlled by his previous actions, and therefore there are different varieties of life for enjoying or suffering.

3. The process of approaching Bhagavan is very wonderful. One who is intelligent should accept that process and be satisfied with whatever comes, favorable or unfavorable, by His supreme will.

4. Now you have decided to undertake this process of Yog under the instruction of your mother, just to achieve the mercy of Bhagavan, but in my opinion such austerities are not possible for any ordinary man. It is very difficult to satisfy Bhagavan Vishnu. *Narada Muni was testing Dhruva Maharaja.*

5. For this reason, my dear boy, you should not endeavor for this; it will not be successful. It is better that you go home. When you are grown up, by the mercy of the Hari you will get a chance for these mystic performances. At that time you may execute this function. *Hari, Bhagavan Vishnu, VasudevaKrishna, Ram, Kalki, Narsimha, Vaman, Balaram, Lakshman, Bharat, Shatrughna, Brahman, Bhagavan and many other names refer to Vishnu Tattva or the same person.*

Dhruva was determined, and he remained unfazed by Narada's apparent discouragement. The great sage Nārada told Dhruva Mahārāja, *'The instruction given by your mother, Sunīti, to follow the path Yog is just suitable for you. You should therefore completely absorb yourself in Yog or devotional service of Vasudev[2]. Any person who desires the fruits of the four principles Dharma (religiosity as per Vedas), Artha (economic development), Kaam (sense gratification) and, at the end, Moksha (liberation or salvation from Karma cycle), should engage himself in the Yog of Hari, for the worship of His lotus feet yields the fulfillment of all of these. My dear boy, I therefore wish all good fortune for you. You should go to the bank of the Yamunā, where there is a virtuous forest named Madhuvana to be purified. Just by going there, one draws nearer Hari, who always lives there.*

My dear boy, in the waters of the Yamunā River, which is known as Kālindī, you should take three baths daily because the water is very auspicious, sacred and clear. After bathing, you should perform the necessary regulative principles for aṣṭāṅga-yog or Hatha Yog and then sit down on your āsana[3] [sitting place] in a calm and quiet position. Bhagavan Vishnu is further described as having the mark of Śrīvatsa, or the sitting place of Lakshmi, and His bodily hue is deep bluish. He is a person, He wears a garland of flowers, and He is eternally manifest with four hands, which hold [beginning from the lower left hand] a conch shell, wheel, club and lotus flower. The entire body of the Supreme Personality of Godhead, Vāsudeva, is decorated. He wears a valuable jeweled helmet, necklaces and bracelets, His neck is adorned with the Kaustubha jewel, and He is dressed in yellow silk garments.'

Then, Narada gave Dhruva the mantra to worship Hari. *This mantra must only be received from a Guru who is in the discipline succession in a sampradaya.*

ॐ नमो भगवते वासुदेवाय ।

When Dhruva Mahārāja, the son of the King, was thus advised by the great sage Nārada, he circumambulated Nārada, his Guru, and offered him respectful obeisances. Then he started for Madhuvana, which is always imprinted with the lotus footprints of Hari and which is therefore especially auspicious.

There Dhruva Maharaja performed austerities on the banks of river Kalindi.

Narada, the Guru of Prahalad

Prahalad was instructed by Narada when he was in the womb of his mother. This is a fascinating story. When Hiranyakashipu had gone to Mandarachal[49] mountain to conduct severe penances, the devatas led by Indra defeated his armies and captured his wife who was carrying his child, Prahlad in the womb. Narada, being the omniscient sage, came to the rescue of the mother from Indra. He told Indra that the child living in the womb is a great devotee of Hari and you won't be able to kill him. So, you should leave this mother and her child with me in my ashram. Prahald told his friends that Narada gave instructions to me and my mother on topics of Krishna and devotional service to Krishna. And those instructions became the basis of his unflinching faith in Krishna. Narada told his friends that even children can understand Krishna if they have the mercy of a Guru like Narada.

Prahlada's teachings to his young friends can be summarized as :

1. Just as the fruits and flowers of a tree in due course of time undergo six changes — birth, existence, growth, transformation, dwindling and then death — the material body, which is obtained by the spirit soul under different circumstances, undergoes similar changes. However, there are no such changes for the spirit soul.

2. "Ātmā" refers to the Supreme Lord or the living entities. Both of them are spiritual, free from birth and death, free

from deterioration and free from material contamination. They are individuals, they are the knowers of the external body, and they are the foundation or shelter of everything. They are free from material change, they are self-illuminated, they are the cause of all causes, and they are all-pervading. They have nothing to do with the material body, and therefore they are always uncovered. With these transcendental qualities, one who is actually learned must give up the illusory conception of life, in which one thinks, "I am this material body, and everything in relationship with this body is mine."

3. An expert geologist can understand where there is gold and by various processes can extract it from the gold ore. Similarly, a spiritually advanced person can understand how the spiritual particle exists within the body, and thus by cultivating spiritual knowledge he can attain perfection in spiritual life. However, as one who is not an expert cannot understand where there is gold, a foolish person who has not cultivated spiritual knowledge cannot understand how the spirit exists within the body.

4. Krishna's eight separated material energies, the three modes of material nature and the sixteen transformations [the eleven senses and the five gross material elements like earth and water] — within all these, the one spiritual soul exists as the observer. Therefore all the great teachers have concluded that the individual soul is conditioned by these material elements.

5. There are two kinds of bodies for every individual soul — a gross body made of five gross elements and a subtle body made of three subtle elements. Within these bodies, however, is the spirit soul. One must find the soul by analysis, saying, "This is not it. This is not it." Thus one must separate spirit from matter.

6. Intelligence can be perceived in three states of activity — wakefulness, dreaming and deep sleep.

7. Surrender to Krishna is the ultimate goal of one's life.

Narada's relationship with Krishna

Even though Krishna is Bhagavan, He sets a great example for the world to follow. *Nowadays, political leaders have no respect for Gurus and Acharyas. Or they do show respect to only those Gurus who do not question them.* One day Narada Muni decided to see the wonder of Bhagavan Krishna marrying sixteen thousand princesses. Without informing Bhagavan Krishna, Narada Muni decided to test the potencies of BHagavan Krishna. *Narada Muni suddenly entered the palace of Rukmini where Bhagavan Krishna was sitting with Rukmini. Bhagavan Krishna greeted Narada Muni in an exemplary manner. As mentioned in Bhagavat Puran,* 'तस्यावनिज्य चरणौ तदपः स्वमूर्ध्नि बिभ्रज्जगद्गुरुतमोऽपि सतां पतिर्हि । ब्रह्मण्यदेव इति यदुगणनाम युक्तं तस्यैव यच्चरणशौचमशेषतीर्थम् ॥ १५ ॥ सम्पूज्य देवऋषिवर्यमृषिः पुराणो नारायणो नरसखो विधिनोदितेन । वाण्याभिभाष्य मितयामृतमिष्टया तं प्राह प्रभो भगवते करवाम हे किम् ॥ १६ ॥ - *Bhagavan Krishna bathed Narada's feet and put that water on his own head worshipping him as the topmost of all Gurus (गुरुतम्). Even though Krishna is also known as Brahmananya-Deva, the Deva of all Brahmanas, He took the water that washed the feet of Narada on his* head. *Even though the water that washes the feet of Krishna becomes Ganga, still He takes the water that washed the feet of Narada Muni on His own head. Then He asked Narada Muni in a very sweet voice - What can we do for you?' Bhagavan Krishna was teaching the way to honor great personalities such as Narada Muni. In Vedas, the word Deva is reserved for Vishnu. His followers are called Devata or Devi or Sura.*

Thus Śrī Kṛṣṇa honored the sage Nārada by bathing his feet, even though the water that bathes the Lord's own feet becomes the Ganges, the ultimate holy shrine. Finally Bhagavan Śrī Nārada said to Krishna: 'श्रीनारद उवाच, नैवाद्भुतं त्वयि विभोऽखिललोकनाथे मैत्री जनेषु सकलेषु दम: खलानाम् । नि:श्रेयसाय हि जगत्स्थितिरक्षणाभ्यां स्वैरावतार उरुगाय विदाम सुष्ठु ॥ १७ ॥दृष्टं तवाङ्घ्रियुगलं जनतापवर्गं ब्रह्मादिभिर्हृदि विचिन्त्यमगाधबोधै: । संसारकूपपतितोत्तरणावलम्बं ध्यायंश्चराम्यनुगृहाण यथा स्मृति: स्यात् ॥ १८ ॥ - Bhagavan, it is no surprise that You, the ruler of all worlds, show friendship for all people and yet subdue the envious. As we well know, You descend by Your sweet will in order to bestow the highest good on this universe by maintaining and protecting it. Thus Your glories are widely sung. Now I have seen Your feet, which grant liberation to Your devotees, which even Brahmā and other great personalities of unfathomable intelligence can only meditate upon within their hearts, and which those who have fallen into the well of material existence resort to for deliverance. Please favor me so that I may constantly think of You as I travel about. Please grant Me the power to remember You.'

This is the only thing that we should ask from Bhagavan Krishna. Then, Narada entered the palace of another queen where Krishna was playing dice with Uddhava. After that Narada entered another palace where he found Krishna was petting His children. In another palace Krishna was preparing to take a bath while in others doing Yagya or even taking remnants of food offered in yagya. In some palaces, Narada found Krishna doing Sandhya Upasana. In some palaces, Narada found Krishna practicing Sword & Shield fighting skills. In some palaces, Krishna was riding on horses, chariots & elephants. In some palaces, Narada found Krishna engaging in water sports. In some other palaces, Narada found Krishna resting on His bed while singers chanted His glories. Narada was traveling at the speed of mind to sixteen thousand palaces made by Krishna for His queens. This opulence of Krishna was shown to Narada Muni because Narada is a bhakt of Bhagavan Krishna. *Without being a bhakt it is not possible to gain favor of Bhagavan Krishna. Narada has all the blessings of Bhagavan Krishna. He is known as Devarshi or Deva amongst Rishis. After visiting Bhagavan Krishna, Narada Muni departed through the sky path to his next destination.* Narada Muni is always traveling to meet new souls to inspire them in Yog. *Yog is Bhakti, and Bhakti is Yog.*

Narada enjoys a loving relationship with Krishna who is his worshipable deity and also a refuge. *Krishna is always kind & loving towards those who follow Dharma and sincerely try to serve Dharma in this world. Narada Muni is His bhakta. Therefore, Narada Muni is considered & respected as one of the foremost Gurus representing Dharma.*

Narada, the Supreme Guru of all Lokpals

Narada is the most misunderstood personality from Vedic scriptures. Oftentimes Narada is depicted as a comic character by Indian movies and television serials. Most of the time, Narada is considered as a Mythological character with no seriousness attributed to his teachings. This Mischaracterization of Narada will be eternally stopped in this book of political science by Narada Muni. The character and wisdom of Narada knows no bounds.

The word Muni in Vedic scriptures is used for thinkers and scientists. Muni is a title which is carefully given to practitioners. Maharishi is used for spiritual practitioners and realized leaders. Maharshi is never used casually for anyone. Maharshi is a title which is carefully given after due consideration. Not everyone can be called Muni or maharshi. Narada is a living being with supernatural powers. He is real and easily accessible through a mediational process. Narada is acclaimed as a Muni in all Vedic traditions. He has been the topmost thinker and social reformer for human mankind.

Narada is also a space traveler because of the divine powers given to him by his father Brahma. *Narada can travel at will to any of the fourteen planetary systems or 'lokas'. The west only knows one where most of the humans live. However, Vedas and Purana give very accurate information about other planetary systems.* Narada was born to a humble maid servant who served a group of spiritually advanced Yogis. Narada in his childhood got a chance to hear those spiritual discourses while living amongst them. Narada tells about himself to Vyasadeva, 'I was born as the son of a certain maidservant engaged in the service of brāhmaṇas who were following the principles of Vedānta[12]. When they were living together during the four months of the rainy season, I was engaged in their personal service. Although they were impartial by nature, those followers of the Vedānta blessed me with their causeless mercy. As far as I was concerned, I was self-controlled and had no attachment to sports, even though I was a boy. In addition, I was not naughty, and I did not speak more than required.' *Without humble service and submissive humble attitude, it is not possible to learn from advanced yogis.*

Narada Continued speaking with Vyasadeva[13], 'Once only, by their permission, I took the remnants of their food, and by doing so all my sins were at once eradicated. Thus being engaged, I became purified in heart, and at that time the very nature of the transcendentalist became attractive to me. In that divine association of saints and by the mercy of those great Vedāntists[50], I could hear them describe the attractive activities of Bhagavan Krishna. And thus listening attentively, my taste for hearing about Hari[14] increased at every step.' *Generally, food tasted by others becomes unfit for consumption because of various*

Karmic and cleanliness regulations. But remnants of foods tasted by great yogis are highly recommended for spiritual growth.

Narada continued, 'O great sage, as soon as I got a taste of bhakti through that service, my attention to hear of Bhagavan Hari was unflinching. And as my taste developed, I realized that it was only in my ignorance that I had accepted gross and subtle coverings, for both Bhagavan and I are transcendental. Thus during two seasons — the rainy season and autumn — I had the opportunity to hear these great-souled sages constantly chant the unadulterated glories of Hari.' *Taste in Bhakti develops only after receiving the mercy of a great Yogi. Yogi just doesn't mean a person who does Asana. Asana is only one aspect of Yog. All advanced souls cannot advance in their spiritual practices without Yog.*

Narada Continued, 'As the flow of my devotional service began, the coverings of the modes of passion and ignorance vanished. I was very much attached to those sages. I was gentle in behavior, and all my sins were eradicated in their service. In my heart I had strong faith in them. I had subjugated the senses, and I was strictly following them with body and mind. As they were leaving, those bhakti-vedāntas[47], who are very kind to poor-hearted souls, instructed me in that most confidential subject which was instructed by Hari Himself.' *Advanced Yogis are Vendantists or who understand Vedanta. Advanced Yogis will impart knowledge to you only when they are pleased with your attitude. If there is a potentiality of misuse, then, Vedantists won't impart knowledge to that person.*

Narada continued, 'By that confidential knowledge, I could clearly understand the influence of the energy of Bhagavan Krishna, the creator, maintainer and annihilator of everything. By knowing that, one can return to Him and personally meet Him. While performing duties according to the order of Bhagavan Shri Krishna, one constantly remembers Him, His names and His qualities.

ॐ नमो भगवते तुभ्यं वासुदेवाय धीमहि ।

प्रद्युम्नायानिरुद्धाय नम: सङ्कर्षणाय च ॥ ३७ ॥

Let us all chant the glories of Vāsudeva[15] along with His plenary expansions Pradyumna[16], Aniruddha[17] and Saṅkarṣaṇa[18]. Thus he is the actual seer who worships, in the form of transcendental sound representation, the Bhagavan[19], Viṣṇu[20], who has no material form.'

This incident shaped his young mind towards yog. After the untimely death of his mother, his only guardian, he decided to continue serving those spiritual scholars. With the knowledge gained due to his spiritual association, he cultivated leaders who help in the social upliftment of all walks of society. After the demise of his mother, Narada Muni walked towards the northern direction. *After leaving his body he attained a new body from Brahma which enabled him to travel freely across all fourteen planetary systems, including Vaikuntha which is far away from all lokas.*

The legendary qualities of Narada Muni for which he is respected all over the three lokas are :

1. Scholar in all branches of Vedas & Upanishads

2. Worshiped by all Devatas

3. Knower of all Itihas (Mahabharat) and Puranas

4. Specialist on the history during previous day of Brahma

5. Expert on Nyaya (logic & reasoning)

6. Expert on essence of Dharma

7. Expert on Shiksha (education), Kalpa (time), Vyakaran (sanskrit grammar), Nirukt (special type of composition), Chhand (special composition) and Jyotish (astrology)

8. Specialist on Aikya (ऐक्य - resolving apparently contradicting Vedic statements) and Samyogananatva (संयोगनानात्व - logically separating mixed sentences)

9. Expert in all types of Yagyas

10. Ability to remember everything spoken once

11. Expert in all matters of policy

12. Ability to see past, present and future

13. Knower of Aparabrahm as well as Parabrahma

14. Ability to reach principle through evidences

15. Expert in analyzing five aspects of speech - Pratigya (statement), Hetu (reason), Udaharan (example), Upanaya (confirmation of Hetu), Nigaman (confirmation)

16. Ability to see all fourteen Lokas

17. Knower of all divisions of Sankhya and Yog

18. Always willing to develop Vairagya in Devatas (who follow Vedas) as well as Asuras (those who do not follow Vedas)

19. Expert in understanding importance of unity as well as division as per time, place & circumstance

20. Expert in determining the strength & weaknesses of enemies

21. Expert in dividing & defeating enemies through diplomacy - Sandhi (संधि - friendship), Vigraha (विग्रह - division), Yaan (यान - attack), Asana (आसन - maintaining silence), Dvaidhibhav (द्वैधिभाव - making enemies fight against one another), and Samashraya (समाश्रय - merger of stronger country)

22. Expert in art of Music

23. Expert in science of warfare

24. Expert in all Vedic knowledge (there is no knowledge outside of Vedas)

25. Freedom from all anger

26. Grave thinker personality

27. Always to the point

28. Trains qualified children in various Vedic sciences

29. A meta physics scientist par excellence

30. Loyal to Vedas and Hari

31. Guru to all famous Vedic personalities

32. Humility personified

33. Intelligence personified

34. Spiritual Analyst

35. Keynote speaker of Devatas

36. Loved by both Sura and Asura

37. The inspiration behind Bhagavata Purana, the spotless purana

38. The world's first preacher of Vedas

39. Devata amongst spiritual monks and ascetics

40. Son of Brahma

41. A gentle, soft spoken and very analytical
42. Speaker par excellence
43. Respected by all in all circumstances
44. Giver of boons
45. Guru of all Kings
46. Best Guide for all humans (manushya)
47. Author of Narada Pancharatra which details the process of deity worship
48. Expert of Artha shastra
49. Expert of political science
50. Expert of Logic and reasoning
51. A space traveler with divine access to the entire creation within the three worlds
52. Original author of Pancharatrika, a treatise on Deity Worship

The fifty two qualities of Narada Muni are the maximum that any living entity can attain through Yog perfection. *Generally a perfected living being can only attain fifty qualities in Toto.* Narada is also the Guru of all Devatas. He is the main teacher of Mahabharat to all Devatas. *Devatas were given three million Shlokas of Mahabharat by Narada Muni.* Narada Muni serves as a messenger of good-will to every living being on all fourteen planetary systems known as Loka. *Sometimes, in order to expedite the Avatar of Vishnu to descend, he creates situations through which the Asuras are annihilated. Asuras always try to destroy the Sura population. Asuras are those who go against the conclusion of Vedas while Suras are those who live according to Vedas. For a common person the difference can be summarized as Suras are law abiding whereas Asuras are generally law breakers. The law is known as*

Dharma which is based on Vedas. This is confirmed in multiple Puranas as well as Vedas.

To hasten Krishna's appearance, Narada instigated Kamsa by informing him of his impending death at the hands of the eight-child of Devaki & Vasudeva. To hasten Narsimha's appearance, Narada protected the child of Hiranyakashipu from Indra. To hasten Vishnu's appearance, Narada gave direction to Dhruv. To punish Paundraka, Narada informed him of the omnipotence of Krishna. To glorify Bhagavan Ram, Narada inspired Valmiki about Shri Ram so that Valmiki Ramayan is written for the benefit of all fourteen lokas (places of residence for living beings). *Narada serves as the Guru of the entire world by constantly chanting the Harinam for the ultimate benefit of all populations.* Narada's conversations with Brahma, Shiva and Vishnu forms the basis of knowledge disseminated to humanity in a simple understandable language.

Lokpal, Loktantra, Loksangraha

LokPal is a Sanskrit word that means maintainer of all living beings. In Vedic histories all Statesmen are called Lokpal because that is the essential duty of a statesman. Lokpal title is officially granted to the Head of State, Head of Government or King. The word Lokpal can also be used generally for some ministers and popular heads of provinces. *As per Puranas, Nearly every single Prince in the ancient past was trained by Narada Muni before that prince ascended their ancestral or elected throne.* Every single head of State should be ideally called as LokPal.

Loksangraha is the philosophy of governance mentioned in Manusmriti, Mahabharat as well as Ramayan. *Chanakya's Arthashastra actually shows the way of Loksangraha. As stated by Bhagavan Krishna in Bhagavad Gita,* 'कर्मणैव हि संसिद्धिमास्थिता जनकादयः । लोकसङ्ग्रहमेवापि सम्पश्यन्कर्तुमर्हसि ॥ २० ॥ - *Great Kings such as Janaka & others attained perfection simply through their activities of Loksangraha. Considering their activities carefully, do what pleases you.' Janaka was known for creating a people friendly government.* Loksangraha means that the government exists for the benefit of the people that it governs. *Loksangraha is neither a socialistic model, nor a capitalistic model. Loksangraha is the philosophy of governance.* Lokassangraha actually means that the government must work towards uplifting the economic, social and Dharmic awareness of the people. Changradupta's government worked on this principle of Lokasangraha. Many kings such as Marthand Varma and Krishnadeva Raya also followed this philosophy of governance. Cholas, Guptas, Chalukyas also used this philosophy of governance. *The western philosophy of governance creates a layer between people and their representatives. The representatives automatically earn a superior status in the society by virtue of their position, influence & power.*

To implement the philosophy of Lokasangraha, a Lokatantra is created. *Tantra means a process or a system.* Loktantra means a system of governance for the benefit of loka (everyone in a country). *Loktantra is a system for implementing Lokasangraha. Loktantra might well be the next phase of evolution for the western democracy.* The major difference between a democracy and loktantra is 'accountability'. In Loktantra strict checks & balances are kept on the representatives of the government. *The western model of democracy allows corruption to flourish through indirect means.* However, in Loktantra, corruption is completely eliminated through extensive training on governance right from the birth of a child. The schools, parents and teachers train the child in logic, reasoning, warfare and Dharma from the very birth to prepare that child for future political leadership.

This child could become the leader in a local area or may even become the head of state. *Just like we train doctors, engineers and even artists, why our society doesn't train politicians?* During the grooming of that child, a special emphasis is given on teaching Vedas, Puranas and Ramayan. That child is observed and tested throughout his student life by his teachers as well as the general public. *If any type of weakness whether be it physical, mental or emotional is found then that child is given other training.* In loktantra, a child is trained right from birth to assume political leadership at local, state or country level in future. The topics of training are:

1. Weapons handling
2. Nyaya (logical reasoning)
3. Niti (policy)
4. Social Interaction (public speaking, training to understand people sentiments)
5. Seven Solutions to manage opponents
6. Establishing Panchayat based governance
7. Thorough knowledge of various topics related to governance in Ramayana and Mahabharat

Most of the content of political courses in Universities are masked by the immature western model of governance. Therefore, such courses are rendered useless for all practical purposes in most regions of the world outside the west. The laziness of academics in non-western countries have contributed to this international malaise. There is a need for new content on the topics of governance. As kalyug progresses, there will be more social unrest sponsored by the west in the name of democracy.

In Loktantra, even an elected official of Panchayat doesn't carry any special privileges any more than any other citizen. The officials are selected based on their qualifications by the most senior Yogi who has no worldly interest other than serving every living being as well as the environment for the purpose of his Yog. The qualifications of such as Yogi are: 'विद्याविनयसम्पन्ने ब्राह्मणे गवि हस्तिनि । शुनि चैव श्वपाके च पण्डिता: समदर्शिन: ॥ १८ ॥' - 'By virtue of true knowledge & humility borne out of practice of Yog, that person sees Brahmana (educated & spiritually advanced person), cow, elephant, dog and even a dog-eater with equal vision.' Nine qualities of such electors are: शमो

दमस्तप: शौचं क्षान्तिरार्जवमेव च । ज्ञानं विज्ञानमास्तिक्यं ब्रह्मकर्म स्वभावजम् ॥

४२ ॥ - 'Peacefulness, complete control of his senses, inclination towards severe austerities, cleanliness, tolerance, honesty, knowledge, wisdom and knowledge of Dharma (as mentioned in Vedas) are the natural qualities of such a person.'

Temples are the major centers of Education, culture, language and business in Loktantra. LokPal, who is the custodian of Loktantra, uses temples to spread language, culture, education, health and wealth.

Yudhishthir's Governance

While living in Indraprastha, with due blessings of Bhishma and Dhritarashtra, Maharaja Yudhishthir and his brothers killed many of their enemies through their military operations. Most citizens of Indraprastha were living happily under the protection of Maharaja Yudhishthir. *Their opulence was compared to a favorable birth obtained after performing good karma in their previous lives. The citizens of Indraprastha were actually grateful to be living under the reign of Maharaja Yudhishthir. Nowadays, the society is perpetually under chaos because good leaders are easily replaced through the power of money in a democracy.*

Yudhishthir had made Dharma (धर्म - rule of law), Arth (अर्थ - Economic prosperity) and Kaam (काम - Opportunities for sense-enjoyment as per Dharma) as cornerstone of his governance policy (नीति - policy). *Citizens need a balanced governance where all their material needs are taken care of. Once Dharma, Artha and Kaam are properly balanced then the desire for the fourth goal of life namely*

Moksha (मोक्ष - freedom from bondage of Karma) automatically arises. Maharaja Yudhishthir himself became an example of moksha because he ruled for the pleasure of Bhagavan Krishna. *Everything that Maharaja Yudhishthir did was considered 'Yukt - युक्त' because everything was done in Yog with Ishwar.*

Citizens received a King in Yudhishthir who was always engaged in thinking about Brahm (ब्रह्म - potency & radiance of Ishwar), performing large Yagyas as per Vedas and eager to use military power to protect all types of residences. *Punishment is the sole prerogative of a lokpal like Yudhishthir. Without the knowledge of Vedas, no leader can actually deliver justice. Justice is always served when the head of state is strong and willing to use force against criminal elements.*

Because of Yudhishthir, the financial condition of all other neighboring states also became stable. *A strong state brings prosperity for all. However, in current times, we often see large powerful countries surrounded by poor countries. For example, all countries towards the south of the USA such as Haiti, Cuba and Mexico are extremely poor. Most countries surrounding China are also extremely poor.* All leaders from other smaller states became wiser due to their association with Maharaja Yudhishthir. Dharma started flourishing in their kingdoms also. *When Dharma is practiced then peace, prosperity and happiness reigns for all.* Yudhishthir was always surrounded by his four brothers who seemed like jewels surrounding a diamond thereby adding further beauty to that diamond.

Maharaja Yudhishthir was surrounded by the great Dhaumya Rishi along with many Brahamanas just like Prajapati Brahma is surrounded by Brihaspati Rishi along with other Devatas. *When a Lokpal respects Brahmanas then he makes good decisions. This also shows the importance of Brahmanas who are well-versed in Vedas and also practicing Yogis to be made chief advisors to the lokpal. When a Lokpal has respect for Brahmanas then that nation can never lose.*

Maharaja Yudhisthir was deeply loved by his citizens. *Citizens would line up to catch a glimpse of Maharaja Yudhisthir. Their eyes would become wet with 'tears of love' and 'tears of happiness' by merely catching a glimpse of Maharaja Yudhishthir.* Citizens were not only merely satisfied by his governance but they also developed deep feelings of attachment & love for him. Maharaja Yudhishthir respected the aspirations of his citizens and he would do everything that would please his citizens. *This is loktantra. Democracy works only for those who control the government. Loktantra works for every citizen. Gradually, the world should move towards loktantra from democracy. Loktantra is better than all political philosophies present today.* Yudhishthir Maharaja always spoke pleasing words and would carefully avoid false promises, loose comments, harsh words, unpleasant words and lies. *He would follow the austerity of speech as mentioned by Bhagavan Krishna in Bhagavad Gita 17.15, 'अनुद्वेगकरं वाक्यं सत्यं प्रियहितं च यत् । स्वाध्यायाभ्यसनं चैव वाङ्मयं तप उच्यते ॥ १५ ॥ - Tapah of speech consists in speaking words that are truthful, pleasing, beneficial, and not agitating to others, and in speaking words that follow the teachings of Vedas.' Svadhyaya means study of Vedic wisdom.* Another good quality of Maharaja Yudhishthir was that he was always happy. He and his brothers not only took care of their own citizens but of all the citizens of other nations who were connected to them through taxes. *Maharaja Yudhishthir would never ask anything from Bhagavan Krishna, Devatas and great rishis for himself. He would always seek their blessings to follow Dharma.*

When Maya (मय) daanav was defeated by Arjun & Bhagavan Krishna, Arjun did not kill him. Because of Arjun, Bhagavan Krishna also forgave him. *That is the power of bhakt or a devotee. Maya daanav offered Arjun anything that Arjun wanted.* Maya Daanav told Arjun, 'I am the Vishwakarma of Danavas. For them, I have built palaces, machines, gardens, waterbodies, different types of weapons, chariots which can move on their own, security towers, boundary walls, large cities with thousands of gates, amazing vehicles including planes and very comfortable tunnels. I also want to do something similar for you.' Arjun replied, 'Because I have given the boon of life to you, I cannot take anything back in return from you.' *Arjun knew the art of daan (दान - loosely translated as charity today) very well. When a reciprocity is expected then that daan becomes a daan in Rajo guna.* Arjun told Maya Daanav, 'I do not want your vow to get wasted and therefore, I ask you to do something for Bhagavan Krishna.' Then, Maya Daanav asked Bhagavan Krishna, 'What can I do for You?' Bhagavan Krishna thought for about forty eight minutes and then told Maya Daanav, 'If you want to do something for Me, then build an assembly hall for Maharaja Yudhishthir. That assembly hall should be so grand that humans may be filled with wonder. Nobody should ever be able to copy that design. That assembly hall should display the prowess & excellence of all of your assistants, Devatas, Asura and even humans in Architecture.' *Maya daanav was very happy to hear the words of Bhagavan Krishna. He decided to make the* assembly hall for Maharaja Yudhishthir which will be like a Vimana (विमान - that which floats).

Bhagavan Krishna and Arjun, then introduced Maya Daanav to Maharaja Yudhishthir. Maharaja Yudhishthir received him with full honors. *Maya Daanav told many unbelievable stories about Daityas to Pandavas. After staying with them for many days, Maya Daanav decided to begin construction of the Assembly hall.* He asked Maharaja Yudhishthir to give him a flat raised land which is ten thousand haath (हाथ - 1.5 feet as per Nepali calculation) by ten thousand feet. *The dimensions are absolutely square as per Vaastu. Vaastu is an ancient vedic science of architecture and construction. All pyramids in the world are square in their base. All ancient temples were constructed on square land. Before selecting the land Maya Daanav performed prayers for the land and also gave valuable gifts to thousands of Brahmanas. Then he selected a land which had the effect of all types of seasons. Maya Daanav went to Hiranyashring mountains near Mainak peaks, north of Kailash. From there he brought a special liquified crystal which was used in the construction of the assembly hall. This special liquid was previously under the control of Vrishparva. He also brought a special golden mace which was studded with valuable gems which he gifted to Bhim. He also brought Devdutt conch shell which he gifted to Arjun. The special characteristic of this conch shell was that it brought fear into the hearts of those who heard it.* This special assembly hall had golden trees inside the building.

The assembly hall was a very tall building appearing to be touching the sky surrounded by clouds. It was made with very expensive material and its interior was decorated with rare paintings. This assembly hall was more beautiful than even the

Sudharma assembly hall of Yadavas. It was even more beautiful than Brahma's assembly hall. Eight thousand Kinkar Rakshasas were carrying this assembly hall to wherever they were ordered to take. These rakshasas were very fierce and were always ready to attack if the security of this assembly hall was breached in any way. There was a very beautiful pond in the center of the assembly hall which was filled with golden lotus flowers. The entire assembly hall was filled with rare birds, fishes and tortoises. Very large trees were planted around the assembly hall. Maya Daanav created this beautiful assembly hall in just fourteen months. *Then, Maya Daanav told Arjun, 'There is one flag on this assembly. In the front part of this assembly a Gana named Kinkar will live there. Whenever there is a large sound from the string of your bow, then these Gana will conjoin you with their loud roars.' Then Maya Daanav offered him the chariot of Agnideva drawn by white horses. The flag had a sign of Hanuman with a special feature that the flag would never get entangled in the trees. The special quality of the flag was that it would always fly upwards. That flag would appear in different colors at different times of the day. Then Maya Daanav handed over the assembly hall to Maharaja Yudhishthir.*

Maharaja Yudhishthir gave a feast of varieties of cooked food to ten thousand Brahmanas before he entered his new assembly hall. *The European and Western Indologists have purposefully ignored the varieties of food prepared for this occasion. The world today appears to be much poorer both in taste and grandeur as compared to Maharaja Yudhishthir's era.* Many great rishis such as Asita, Devata, Satya, Sarpimarli, Mahashira, Avarvasu, Sumitra, Maitreya, Sounak, Vyasadeva, Shukadeva, Sumantu, Jaimini, Paila, Tittiri, Yagyavalkya, Dhaumya, Kaushik, Bhrigu, Gautam, Shandilya and many others graced that great assembly regularly. Many other great Kings such as Mahabali Kampan from other parts of the world would also sit in that great assembly. Many other princes were also there who would train under Arjun on warfare. Many great musicians and dancers adorned that great assembly.

One day when Maharaja Yudhishthir was sitting in the assembly along with other great rishis and Gandharvas, Narada Muni who was accompanied by Parijat Muni, Parvat Muni, Saumya Muni, Sumukh Muni & others suddenly arrived. *They all appeared suddenly and immediately began to shower their blessings on Yudhishthir.* Maharaja Yudhishthir and the entire assembly got up from their seats to greet Narada Muni. *They offered their obeisances to Narada Muni cows, madhuparka (special sweet), Arghya and various types of prayers to please him.* Narada Muni was visibly satisfied with the reception and became comfortably situated on a prominent seat vacated by Maharaja Yudhishthir. *All other great personalities took their respective seats while Pandavas led by Maharaja Yudhishthir sat at the feet of Narada Muni.* Narada Muni was visibly pleased by the reception given by Maharaja Yudhishthir and began asking questions on Dharma, Kaam and Artha to Maharaja Yudhishthir.

नारद उवाच

कच्चिदर्थाश्च कल्पन्ते धर्मे च रमते मनः ।
सुखानि चानुभूयन्ते मनश्च न विहन्यते ॥ १७ ॥

...जानकर उस प्रकाशित तो नहीं कर देते ? ॥ २४ ॥
मित्रोदासीनशत्रूणां कच्चिद् वेत्सि चिकीर्षितम् ।
कच्चित् संधिं यथाकालं विग्रहं चोपसेवसे ॥ २५ ॥

क्या तुम मित्र, शत्रु और उदासीन लोगोंके
सम्बन्धमें यह ज्ञान रखते हो कि वे कब क्या करना
चाहते हैं ? उपयुक्त समयका विचार करके ही संधि
और विग्रहकी नीतिका सेवन करते हो न ? ॥ २५ ॥

कच्चिद् वृत्तिमुदासीने मध्यमे चानुमन्यसे ।
कच्चिदात्मसमा वृद्धाः शुद्धाः सम्बोधनक्षमाः ॥ २६ ॥
कुलीनाश्चानुरक्ताश्च कृतास्ते वीर मन्त्रिणः ।
विजयो मन्त्रमूलो हि राज्ञो भवति भारत ॥ २७ ॥

क्या तुम्हें इस बातका अनुमान है कि उदासीन एवं
मध्यम व्यक्तियोंके प्रति कैसा बर्ताव करना चाहिये ?
वीर! तुमने अपने स्वयंके समान विश्वसनीय वृद्ध, शुद्ध
हृदयवाले, किसी बातको अच्छी तरह समझानेमें समर्थ,
उत्तम कुलमें उत्पन्न और अपने प्रति अत्यन्त अनुराग
रखनेवाले पुरुषोंको ही मन्त्री बना रखा है न ? क्योंकि
भारत! राजाको विजयप्राप्तिका मूल कारण अच्छा मन्त्रणा
(सलाह) और उसकी सुरक्षा ही है, (जो सुयोग्य
मन्त्रीके अधीन है।) ॥ २६–२७ ॥

कच्चित् संवृतमन्त्रैस्तैरमात्यैः शास्त्रकोविदैः ।
राष्ट्रं सुरक्षितं तात शत्रुभिर्न विलुप्यते ॥ २८ ॥

तात! मन्त्रको गुप्त रखनेवाले उन शास्त्रज्ञ सचिवोंद्वारा
तुम्हारा राष्ट्र सुरक्षित तो है न ? शत्रुओंद्वारा उसका नाश
तो नहीं हो रहा है ? ॥ २८ ॥

कच्चिन्निद्रावशं नैषि कच्चित् काले विबुध्यसे ।
कच्चिच्चापररात्रेषु   चिन्तयस्यर्थमर्थवित् ॥ २९ ॥

तुम असमयमें ही निद्राके वशीभूत तो नहीं होते ?
समयपर जग जाते हो न ? अर्थशास्त्रके जानकार तो तुम
हो ही। रात्रिके पिछले भागमें जगकर अपने अर्थ
(आवश्यक कर्तव्य एवं हित)–के विषयमें विचार तो
करते हो न ? ॥ २९ ॥

कच्चिन्मन्त्रयसे नैकः कच्चिन बहुभिः सह ।
कच्चित् ते मन्त्रितो मन्त्रो न राष्ट्रं परिधावति ॥ ३० ॥

(कोई भी गुप्त मन्त्रणा दीये चार कानोंतक ही गुप्त
रहती है, छः कानोंमें जाते ही वह फट जाती है। अत...

विचार नहीं करते अथवा बहुत लोगोंके साथ बैठकर
तो मन्त्रणा नहीं करते ? कहीं ऐसा तो नहीं होता कि
तुम्हारी निश्चित की हुई गुप्त मन्त्रणा फूटकर शत्रुके
राज्यतक फैल जाती हो ? ॥ ३० ॥

कच्चिदर्थान्विनिश्चित्य लघुमूलान् महोदयान् ।
क्षिप्रमारभसे कर्तुं न विघ्नयसि तादृशान् ॥ ३१ ॥

धनकी वृद्धिके ऐसे उपायोंका निश्चय करके,
जिनमें मूलधन तो कम लगाना पड़ता हो, किंतु वृद्धि
अधिक होती हो, उनका शीघ्रतापूर्वक आरम्भ कर लेते
हो न ? वैसे कार्योंमें अथवा वैसा कार्य करनेवाले
लोगोंके मार्गमें तुम विघ्न तो नहीं डालते ? ॥ ३१ ॥

कच्चिन्न सर्वे कर्मान्ताः परोक्षास्ते विशङ्कितः ।
सर्वे वा पुनरुत्सृष्टाः संसृष्टं चात्र कारणम् ॥ ३२ ॥

तुम्हारे राज्यके किसान—मजदूर आदि श्रमजीवी
मनुष्य तुमसे अज्ञात तो नहीं हैं ? उनके कार्य और
गतिविधिपर तुम्हारी दृष्टि है न ? वे तुम्हारे अविश्वासके
पात्र तो नहीं हैं अथवा तुम उन्हें बार–बार छोड़ते और
पुनः कामपर लेते तो नहीं रहते ? क्योंकि महान
अभ्युदय या उन्नतिमें उन सबका स्नेहपूर्ण सहयोग
ही कारण है। (क्योंकि चिरकालसे अनुगृहीत होनेपर
ही वे ज्ञात, विश्वासपात्र और स्वामीके प्रति अनुरक्त
होते हैं) ॥ ३२ ॥

आप्तैरनुब्धैः क्रियिकैस्ते च कच्चिदनुष्ठिताः ।
कच्चिद् राजन् कृतान्येव कृतप्रायाणि वा पुनः ॥ ३३ ॥
विदुस्ते वीर कर्माणि नानबाप्तानि कानिचित् ।

कृषि आदिके कार्य विश्वसनीय, लोभरहित और
बड़े–बूढ़ोंके समयसे चले आनेवाले कार्यकर्ताओंद्वारा
ही कराते हो न ? राजन्! वीरशिरोमणे! क्या तुम्हारे
कार्यकी सिद्ध हो जानेपर या सिद्धिके निकट पहुँच
जानेपर ही लोग जान पाते हैं ? सिद्ध होनेसे पहले ही
तुम्हारे किन्हीं कार्योंको लोग जान तो नहीं लेते ? ॥ ३३ ॥

कच्चित् कारणिका धर्मं सर्वशास्त्रेषु कोविदाः ।
कारयन्ति कुमारांश्च योधमुख्यांश्च सर्वशः ॥ ३४ ॥

तुम्हारे यहाँ जो शिक्षा देनेका काम करते हैं, वे
धर्म एवं सम्पूर्ण शास्त्रोंके मर्मज्ञ विद्वान् होकर ही

Original Sanskrit Plate - 1

कश्चित् सहस्त्रैर्मूर्खाणामेकं क्रीणासि पण्डितम्।
पण्डितो ह्यर्थकृच्छ्रेषु कुर्यान्निःश्रेयसं परम्॥ ३५॥
तुम हजारों मूर्खोंके बदले एक पण्डितको ही तो
खरीदते हो न? अर्थात् आदरपूर्वक स्वीकार करते हो
न? क्योंकि विद्वान् पुरुष ही अर्थसंकटके समय महान्
कल्याण कर सकता है॥ ३५॥

कश्चिद् दुर्गाणि सर्वाणि धनधान्यायुधोदकैः।
यन्त्रैश्च परिपूर्णानि तथा शिल्पिधनुर्धरैः॥ ३६॥
क्या तुम्हारे सभी दुर्ग (किले) धन-धान्य, अस्त्र-
शस्त्र, जल, यन्त्र (मशीन), शिल्पी और धनुर्धर
सैनिकोंसे भरे-पूरे रहते हैं? ॥ ३६॥

एकोऽप्यमात्यो मेधावी शूरो दान्तो विचक्षणः।
राजानं राजपुत्रं वा प्रापयेन्महतीं श्रियम्॥ ३७॥
यदि एक भी मन्त्री मेधावी, शौर्यसम्पन्न, संयमी
और चतुर हो तो राजा अथवा राजकुमारको विपुल
सम्पत्तिको प्राप्ति करा देता है॥ ३७॥

कच्चिद्दष्टादशान्येषु स्वपक्षे दश पञ्च च।
त्रिभिस्त्रिभिरविज्ञातैर्वेत्सि तीर्थानि चारकैः॥ ३८॥
क्या तुम शत्रुपक्षके अठारह और अपने पक्षके
पंद्रह तीर्थोंकी तीन-तीन अज्ञात गुप्तचरोंद्वारा देख-
भाल या जाँच-पड़ताल करते रहते हो? ॥ ३८॥

कच्चिद् द्विषामविदितः प्रतिपन्नश्च सर्वदा।
नित्ययुक्तो रिपून् सर्वान् वीक्षसे रिपुसूदन॥ ३९॥
शत्रुसूदन! तुम शत्रुओंसे अज्ञात, सतत सावधान
और नित्य प्रयत्नशील रहकर अपने सम्पूर्ण शत्रुओंकी
गतिविधिपर दृष्टि रखते हो न? ॥ ३९॥

कच्चिद् विनयसम्पन्नः कुलपुत्रो बहुश्रुतः।
अनसूयनुप्रष्टा सत्कृतस्ते पुरोहितः॥ ४०॥
क्या तुम्हारे पुरोहित विनयशील, कुलीन, बहुश्रुत,
विद्वान्, दोषदृष्टिसे रहित तथा शास्त्रचर्चामें कुशल हैं?
क्या तुम उनका पूर्ण सत्कार करते हो? ॥ ४०॥

कश्चिदग्निषु ते युक्तो विधिज्ञो मतिमानृजुः।
हुतं च होष्यमाणं च काले वेदयते सदा॥ ४१॥
तुमने अग्निहोत्रके लिये विधिज्ञ, बुद्धिमान् और

सरल स्वभावके ब्राह्मणको नियुक्त किया है जो
सदा किये हुए और किये जानेवाले हवनको तुम्हें ठीक
समयपर सूचित कर देता है न?॥ ४१॥

कच्चिदङ्गेषु निष्णातो ज्योतिषः प्रतिपादकः।
उत्पातेषु च सर्वेषु दैवज्ञः कुशलस्तव॥ ४२॥
क्या तुम्हारे यहाँ हस्त-पादादि अंगोंकी परीक्षामें
निपुण, ग्रहोंकी लग्न तथा अतिचार आदि गतियों एवं
उनके शुभाशुभ परिणाम आदिको बतानेवाला तथा
दिव्य, भौम एवं शरीरसम्बन्धी सब प्रकारके उत्पातोंको
पहलेसे ही जान लेनेमें कुशल ज्योतिषी है? ॥ ४२॥

कच्चिन्मुख्या महत्स्वेव मध्यमेषु च मध्यमाः।
जघन्याश्च जघन्येषु भृत्याः कर्मसु योजिताः॥ ४३॥
तुमने प्रधान-प्रधान व्यक्तियोंको उनके योग्य
महान् कार्योंमें, मध्यम श्रेणीके कार्यकर्ताओंको मध्यम
कार्योंमें तथा निम्न श्रेणीके सेवकोंको उनकी योग्यताके
अनुसार छोटे कामोंमें ही लगा रखा है न? ॥ ४३॥

अमात्यानुपधातीतान् पितृपैतामहाञ्छुचीन्।
श्रेष्ठाञ्छ्रेष्ठेषु कच्चित्त्वं नियोजयसि कर्मसु॥ ४४॥
क्या तुम निश्छल, बाप-दादोंके क्रमसे चले आये
हुए और पवित्र आचार-विचारवाले श्रेष्ठ मन्त्रियोंको
सदा श्रेष्ठ कर्मोंमें लगाये रखते हो? ॥ ४४॥

कच्चिन्नोग्रेण दण्डेन भृशमुद्विजसे प्रजाः।
राष्ट्रं तवानुशासन्ति मन्त्रिणो भरतर्षभ॥ ४५॥
भरतश्रेष्ठ! कठोर दण्डके द्वारा तुम प्रजाजनोंको
अत्यन्त उद्वेगमें तो नहीं डाल देते? तुम्हारे मन्त्रीलोग
राष्ट्रका न्यायपूर्वक पालन करते हैं न? ॥ ४५॥

कच्चित्त्वां नावजानन्ति याजकाः पतितं यथा।
उग्रप्रतिग्रहीतारं कामयानमिव स्त्रियः॥ ४६॥
जैसे पतिव्रता याजक पतित यजमानको और स्त्रियाँ
कामचारी पुरुषको तिरस्कार कर देती हैं, उसी प्रकार
प्रजा कठोरतापूर्वक अधिक कर लेनेके कारण तुम्हारा
अनादर तो नहीं करती? ॥ ४६॥

कच्चिद्धृष्टश्च शूरश्च मतिमान् धृतिमाञ्छुचिः।
कुलीनश्चानुरक्तश्च दक्षः सेनापतिस्तथा॥ ४७॥

Original Sanskrit Plate - 2

तथा अपने कार्यमें कुशल है ?॥ ४७ ॥
कच्चिद् बलस्य ते मुख्याः सर्वयुद्धविशारदाः ।
धृष्टावदाता विक्रान्तास्त्वया सत्कृत्य मानिताः ॥ ४८ ॥
तुम्हारी सेनाके मुख्य-मुख्य दलपति सब प्रकारके युद्धोंमें चतुर, धृष्ट (निर्भय), निष्कपट और पराक्रमी हैं न? तुम उनका यथोचित सत्कार एवं सम्मान करते हो न ?॥ ४८ ॥
कच्चिद् बलस्य भक्तं च वेतनं च यथोचितम् ।
सम्प्राप्तकाले दातव्यं ददासि न विकर्षसि ॥ ४९ ॥
अपनी सेनाके लिये यथोचित भोजन और वेतन ठीक समयपर दे देते हो न? जो उन्हें दिया जाना चाहिये, उसमें कमी या विलम्ब तो नहीं कर देते ?॥ ४९ ॥
कालातिक्रमणादेते भक्तवेतनयोर्भृताः ।
भर्तुः कुप्यन्ति यद्भृत्याः सोऽनर्थः सुमहान् स्मृतः ॥ ५० ॥
भोजन और वेतनमें अधिक विलम्ब होनेपर भृत्यगण अपने स्वामीपर कुपित हो जाते हैं और उनका वह कोप महान् अनर्थका कारण बताया गया है॥ ५० ॥
कच्चिद् सर्वेऽनुरक्तास्त्वां कुलपुत्राः प्रधानतः ।
कच्चित् प्राणांस्तवार्थेषु संत्यजन्ति सदा युधि ॥ ५१ ॥
क्या उत्तम कुलमें उत्पन्न मन्त्री आदि सभी प्रधान अधिकारी तुमसे प्रेम रखते हैं? क्या वे युद्धमें तुम्हारे हितके लिये अपने प्राणोंतकका त्याग करनेको सदा तैयार रहते हैं ?॥ ५१ ॥
कच्चिन्नैको बहुनर्थान् सर्वेशः साम्परायिकान् ।
अनुशास्ति यथाकामं कायात्मा शासनातिगः ॥ ५२ ॥
तुम्हारे कर्मचारियोंमें कोई ऐसा तो नहीं है, जो अपनी इच्छाके अनुसार चलनेवाला और तुम्हारी शासनका उल्लंघन करनेवाला हो तथा युद्धके सारे साधनों एवं कार्योंको अकेला ही अपनी रुचिके अनुसार चला रहा हो ?॥ ५२ ॥
कच्चित् पुरुषकारेण पुरुषः कर्म शोभयन् ।
लभते मानमधिकं भूयो वा भक्तवेतनम् ॥ ५३ ॥
(तुम्हारे यहाँ काम करनेवाला) कोई पुरुष अपने पुरुषार्थसे जब किसी कार्यको अच्छे ढंगसे सम्पन्न

कच्चिद् विद्याविनीतांश्च नराञ्ज्ञानविशारदान् ।
यथार्हं गुणतश्चैव दानेनाभ्युपपद्यसे ॥ ५४ ॥
क्या तुम विद्यासे विनयशील एवं ज्ञानिन् मनुष्योंको उनके गुणोंके अनुसार यथायोग्य धन आदि देकर उनका सम्मान करते हो ?॥ ५४ ॥
कच्चिद् दाराश्च नुष्याणां तवार्थं मृत्युमीयुषाम् ।
व्यसनं चाभ्युपेतानां बिभर्षि भरतर्षभ ॥ ५५ ॥
भरतश्रेष्ठ! जो लोग तुम्हारे हितके लिये संत मृत्युका वरण कर लेते हैं अथवा भारी संकटमें पड़ जाते हैं, उनके बाल-बच्चोंकी रक्षा तुम करते हो न ?॥ ५५ ॥
कच्चिद् भयादुपगतं क्षीणं वा रिपुमागतम् ।
युद्धे वा विजितं पार्थ पुत्रवत् परिरक्षसि ॥ ५६ ॥
कुन्तीनन्दन! जो भयसे अथवा अपनी धन-सम्पत्तिका नाश होनेसे तुम्हारी शरणमें आया हो या युद्धमें तुमसे परास्त हो गया हो, ऐसे शत्रुका तुम पुत्रके समान पालन करते हो या नहीं ?॥ ५६ ॥
कच्चित् त्वमेव सर्वस्याः पृथिव्याः पृथिवीपते ।
समश्चानभिशङ्क्यश्च यथा माता यथा पिता ॥ ५७ ॥
पृथिवीपते! क्या समस्त भूमण्डलकी प्रजा तुम्हें ही समदर्शी एवं माता-पिताके समान विश्वसनीय मानती है ?॥ ५७ ॥
कच्चिद् व्यसनिनं शत्रुं निशम्य भरतर्षभ ।
अभियासि जवेनैव समीक्ष्य त्रिविधं बलम् ॥ ५८ ॥
भरतकुलभूषण! क्या तुम अपने शत्रुको (द्यूत आदि) दुर्व्यसनोंमें फँसा हुआ सुनकर उसके त्रिविध बल (मन्त्र, कोष एवं भृत्य-बल अथवा प्रभुशक्ति, मन्त्रशक्ति एवं उत्साहशक्ति)-पर विचार करके यदि वह दुर्बल हो तो उसके ऊपर बड़े वेगसे आक्रमण कर देते हो ?॥ ५८ ॥
यात्रायारम्भे दिष्टश्च प्राप्तकालमरिंदम ।
पार्ष्णिमूलं च विज्ञाय व्यवसायात् पराजयम् ।
बलस्य च महाराज दत्त्वा वेतनमग्रतः ॥ ५९ ॥

Original Sanskrit Plate - 3

निश्चय करके और पराजयमूलक क्याससोंका अपने पक्षमें अभाव तथा शत्रुपक्षमें आधिक्य देखकर उचित अवसर आनेपर दैवका भरोसा करके अपने सैनिकोंको अग्रिम वेतन देकर शत्रुपर चढ़ाई कर देते हो ?॥ ५९ ॥

कच्चिच्च बलमुख्येभ्यः परराष्ट्रे परंतप।
उपच्छन्नानि रत्नानि प्रयच्छसि यथार्हतः ॥ ६० ॥

परंतप ! शत्रुके राज्यमें जो प्रधान-प्रधान योद्धा हैं, उन्हें छिपे-छिपे यथायोग्य रत्न आदि भेंट करते रहते हो या नहीं ?॥ ६० ॥

कच्चिदात्मानमेवाग्रे विजित्य विजितेन्द्रियः।
परान् जिगीषसे पार्थ प्रमत्तानजितेन्द्रियान्॥ ६१ ॥

कुन्तीनन्दन! क्या तुम पहले अपनी इन्द्रियों और मनको जीतकर ही प्रमादमें पड़े हुए अजितेन्द्रिय शत्रुओंको जीतनेकी इच्छा करते हो ?॥ ६१ ॥

कच्चिद् ते सास्यतः शत्रून् पूर्व यान्ति स्वनुष्ठिताः।
साम दानं च भेदश्च दण्डश्च विधिवद् गुणाः ॥ ६२ ॥

शत्रुओंपर तुम्हारे आक्रमण करनेसे पहले अच्छी तरह प्रयोगमें लाये हुए तुम्हारे साम, दान, भेद और दण्ड—ये चार गुण विधिपूर्वक उन शत्रुओंतक पहुँच जाते हैं या न ? (क्योंकि शत्रुओंको वशमें करनेके लिये इनका प्रयोग आवश्यक है।) ॥ ६२ ॥

कच्चिन्मूलं दृढं कृत्वा परान् यासि विशाम्पते।
तांश्च विक्रमसे जेतुं जित्वा च परिरक्षसि ॥ ६३ ॥

महाराज! तुम अपने राज्यकी नींवको दृढ़

कच्चिदष्टाङ्गसंयुक्ता चतुर्विधबला चमूः।
बलमुख्यैः सुनीता ते द्विषतां प्रतिवर्धिनी ॥ ६४ ॥

क्या धनरक्षक, द्रव्यसंग्राहक, चिकित्सक, गुप्तचर, पाचक, सेवक, लेखक और प्रहरी—इन आठ अंगों और हाथी, घोड़े, रथ एवं पैदल—इन चार प्रकारके बलोंसे युक्त तुम्हारी सेना सुयोग्य सेनापतियोंद्वारा अच्छी तरह संचालित होकर शत्रुओंका संहार करनेमें समर्थ होती है ?॥

कच्चिल्लवं च मुष्टिं च परराष्ट्रे परंतप।
अविहाय महाराज निहंसि समरे रिपून्॥ ६५ ॥

शत्रुओंको संतप्त करनेवाले महाराज! तुम शत्रुओंके राज्यमें अन्नाज काटने और दुर्भिक्षके समयकी उपेक्षा न करके रणभूमिमें शत्रुओंको मारते हो न ?॥ ६५ ॥

कच्चित् स्वपरराष्ट्रेषु बहवोऽधिकृतास्तव।
अर्थान् समधितिष्ठन्ति रक्षन्ति च परस्परम्॥ ६६ ॥

क्या अपने और शत्रुके राष्ट्रोंमें बहुत-से अधिकारी स्थान-स्थानमें घूम-फिरकर प्रजाको वशमें करने एवं कर लेने आदि प्रयोजनोंको सिद्ध करते हैं और परस्पर मिलकर राष्ट्र एवं अपने पक्षके लोगोंकी रक्षामें लगे रहते हैं ?॥ ६६ ॥

कच्चिदभ्यवहार्याणि गात्रसंस्पर्शनानि च।
घ्रेयाणि च महाराज रक्षन्त्यनुमतास्तव॥ ६७ ॥

महाराज! तुम्हारे खाद्य पदार्थ, शरीरसे धारण करनेके वस्त्र आदि तथा सूँघनेके उपयोगमें आनेवाले सुगन्धित द्रव्योंकी रक्षा विश्वस्त पुरुष ही करते हैं न ?॥ ६७ ॥

कच्चित् कोषश्च कोष्ठं च वाहनं द्वारमायुधम्।
आयश्च कृतकल्याणैस्तव भक्तैरनुष्ठितः ॥ ६८ ॥

Original Sanskrit Plate - 4

कच्चिदाभ्यन्तरेभ्यश्च बाह्येभ्यश्च विशाम्यते।
रक्षस्यात्मानमेवाग्रे तांश्च स्वेभ्यो मिथश्च तान्॥ ६१॥

प्रजापालक नरेश! क्या तुम रसोइये आदि भीतरी सेवकों तथा सेनापति आदि बाह्य सेवकोंद्वारा भी पहले अपनी ही रक्षा करते हो, फिर आत्मीयजनोंद्वारा एवं परस्पर एक-दूसरेसे उन सबको रक्षापर भी ध्यान देते हो?॥ ६१॥

कच्चिन पाने घूते वा क्रीडासु प्रमदासु च।
प्रतिजानन्ति पूर्वाह्णे व्यर्थं व्यसनजं च तव॥ ७०॥

तुम्हारे सेवक पूर्वाह्णकालमें (जो कि धर्माचरणका समय है) तुमसे मद्यपान, घूत, क्रीड़ा और युवती स्त्री आदि दुर्व्यसनोंमें तुम्हारा समय और धनको व्यर्थ नष्ट करनेके लिये प्रस्तुत तो नहीं करते?॥ ७०॥

कच्चिदायस्य चार्धेन चतुर्भागेन वा पुनः।
पादभागैस्त्रिभिर्वापि व्ययः संशुध्यते तव॥ ७१॥

क्या तुम्हारे आयके एक चौथाई या आधे अथवा तीन चौथाई भागसे तुम्हारा सारा खर्च चल जाता है?॥ ७१॥

कच्चिज्ज्ञातीन्गुरून्वृद्धान्वणिजः शिल्पिनः श्रितान्।
अभीक्ष्णमनुगृह्णासि धनधान्येन दुर्गतान्॥ ७२॥

तुम अपने आश्रित कुटुम्बके लोगों, गुरुजनों, बड़े-बूढ़ों, व्यापारियों, शिल्पियों तथा दीन-दुखियोंको धन-धान्य देकर उनपर सदा अनुग्रह करते रहते हो न?॥ ७२॥

कच्चिच्च्याय्यव्यये युक्ताः सर्वे गणकलेखकाः।
अनुतिष्ठन्ति पूर्वाह्णे नित्यमायं व्ययं तव॥ ७३॥

तुम्हारी आमदनी और खर्चकी लिखने और जोड़नेके काममें लगाये हुए सभी लेखक और गणक प्रतिदिन पूर्वाह्णकालमें तुम्हारे सामने अपना हिसाब पेश करते हैं न?॥ ७३॥

कच्चिदर्थेषु सम्प्रौढान् हितकामानुप्रियान्।
नापकर्षसि कर्मभ्यः पूर्वमप्राप्य किल्बिषम्॥ ७४॥

किन्हीं कार्योंमें नियुक्त किये हुए प्रौढ़, हितैषी एवं प्रिय कर्मचारियोंको पहले उनके किसी अपराधको जाँच किये बिना तुम कामसे अलग तो नहीं कर देते हो?॥ ७४॥

कच्चिद् विदित्वा पुरुषानुत्तमाधममध्यमान्।
त्वं कर्मस्वनुरूपेषु नियोजयसि भारत॥ ७५॥

भारत! तुम उत्तम, मध्यम और अधम श्रेणी मनुष्योंको पहचानकर उन्हें उनके अनुरूप कार्यों में लगाते हो न?॥ ७५॥

कच्चिन्न लुब्धाश्चौरा वा वैरिणो वा विशाम्यते।
अप्राप्तव्यवहारा वा तव कर्मस्वनुष्ठिताः॥ ७६॥

राजन्! तुमने ऐसे लोगोंको तो अपने कार्यमें नहीं लगा रखा है? जो लोभी, चोर, शत्रु अथवा व्यावहारिक अनुभवसे सर्वथा शून्य हों?॥ ७६॥

कच्चिन्न चौरैर्लुब्धैर्वा कुमारैः स्त्रीबलेन वा।
त्वया वा पीड्यते राष्ट्रं कच्चित् तुष्टाः कृषीवलाः॥ ७७॥

चोरों, लोभियों, राजकुमारों या राजकुलकी स्त्रियों अथवा स्वयं तुमसे ही तुम्हारे राष्ट्रको पीड़ा तो नहीं रही है? क्या तुम्हारे राज्यके किसान संतुष्ट हैं?॥ ७७॥

कच्चिद् राष्ट्रे तडागानि पूर्णानि च बृहन्ति च।
भागशो विनिविष्टानि न कृषिर्देवमातृका॥ ७८॥

क्या तुम्हारे राज्यके सभी भागोंमें जलसे भरे हुए बड़े-बड़े तालाब बनवाये गये हैं? केवल वर्षा पानीके भरोसे ही तो खेती नहीं होती है?॥ ७८॥

कच्चिन्न भक्तं बीजं च कर्षकस्यावसीदति।
प्रत्येकं च शतं वृद्ध्या ददास्यृणमनुग्रहम्॥ ७९॥

तुम्हारे राज्यके किसानको अन्न या बीज तो मर नहीं होता? क्या तुम प्रत्येक किसानपर अनुग्रह करके उसे एक रुपया सैकड़े ब्याजपर ऋण देते हो?॥ ७९॥

कच्चित् स्वनुष्ठिता तात वार्ता ते साधुभिर्जनैः।
वार्तायां संश्रितस्तात लोकोऽयं सुखमेधते॥ ८०॥

तात! तुम्हारे राष्ट्रमें अच्छे पुरुषोंद्वारा वार्ता—कृषि, गोरक्षा तथा व्यापारका काम अच्छी तरह किया जाता है न? क्योंकि उपर्युक्त वार्तावृत्तिपर अवलम्बित रहनेवाले लोग ही सुखपूर्वक उन्नति करते हैं॥ ८०॥

कच्चिच्छूराः कृतप्रज्ञाः पञ्च पञ्च स्वनुष्ठिताः।
क्षेमं कुर्वन्ति संहत्य राजञ्जनपदे तव॥ ८१॥

राजन्! क्या तुम्हारे जनपदके प्रत्येक गाँवमें शूरवीर, बुद्धिमान् और कार्यकुशल पाँच-पाँच व्यक्ति मिलकर सुचारुरूपसे जनहितके कार्य करते हुए सबका कल्याण करते हैं?॥ ८१॥

कच्चिन्नगरगुप्त्यर्थं ग्रामा नगरवत् कृताः।
ग्रामवच्च कृताः प्रान्तास्ते च सर्वे विदर्पणाः॥ ८२॥
क्या नगरोंकी रक्षाके लिये गाँवोंको भी नगरके ही समान बना ...

Original Sanskrit Plate - 5

कच्चिद् बलेनानुगताः समानि विषमाणि च।
पुराणि चौरान् निघ्नन्तश्चरन्ति विषये तव॥८३॥
क्या तुम्हारे राज्यमें कुछ रक्षक पुरुष सेना साथ
लेकर चोर-डाकुओंका दमन करते हुए सुगम एवं दुर्गम
नगरोंमें विचरते रहते हैं?॥८३॥
कच्चित् स्त्रियः सान्त्वयसि कच्चित् ताश्च सुरक्षिताः।
कच्चिन्न श्रद्धास्यासां कच्चिद् गुह्यं न भाषसे॥८४॥
तुम स्त्रियोंको सान्त्वना देकर संतुष्ट रखते
हो न? क्या वे तुम्हारे यहाँ पूर्णरूपसे सुरक्षित हैं?
तुम उनपर पूरा विश्वास तो नहीं करते? और
विश्वास करके उन्हें कोई गुप्त बात तो नहीं बता
देते?॥८४॥
कच्चिदात्ययिकं श्रुत्वा तदर्थमनुचिन्त्य च।
प्रियाप्यनुभवच्छेषे न त्वमनःपुरे नृप॥८५॥
राजन्! तुम कोई अमंगलसूचक समाचार सुनकर
और उसके विषयमें बार-बार विचार करके भी प्रिय
भोग-विलासोंका आनन्द लेते हुए अन्तःपुरमें ही सोते
तो नहीं रह जाते?॥८५॥
कच्चिद् द्वौ प्रथमौ यामौ रात्रेः सुप्त्वा विशाम्पते।
संचिन्तयसि धर्मार्थौ याम उत्थाय पश्चिमे॥८६॥
प्रजानाथ! क्या तुम रात्रिके (पहले पहरके बाद)
जो प्रथम दो (दूसरे-तीसरे) याम हैं, उन्हींमें सोकर
अंतिम पहरमें उठकर बैठ जाते और धर्म एवं अर्थका
चिंतन करते हो?॥८६॥
कच्चिदर्थयसे नित्यं मनुष्यान् समलंकृतः।
उत्थाय काले कालज्ञैः सह पाण्डव मन्त्रिभिः॥८७॥
पाण्डुनन्दन! तुम प्रतिदिन समयपर उठकर स्नान
आदिके पश्चात् वस्त्राभूषणोंसे अलंकृत हो देश-कालके
ज्ञाता मन्त्रियोंके साथ बैठकर (प्रार्थी या दर्शनार्थी)
मनुष्योंकी इच्छा पूर्ण करते हो न?॥८७॥
कच्चिद् रक्ताम्बरधराः खड्गहस्ताः स्वलंकृताः।
उपासते त्वामभितो रक्षणार्थमरिंदम॥८८॥

रहते हैं?॥८८॥
कच्चिद् दण्ड्येषु यमवत्पृश्येषु च विशाम्पते।
परीक्ष्य वर्तसे सम्यगप्रियेषु प्रियेषु च॥८९॥
महाराज! क्या तुम दण्डनीय अपराधियोंके प्रति
यमराज और पूजनीय पुरुषोंके प्रति धर्मराजका-सा
बर्ताव करते हो? प्रिय एवं अप्रिय व्यक्तियोंकी
भलीभाँति परीक्षा करके ही व्यवहार करते हो न?॥८९॥
कच्चिच्छरीरमाबाधमौषधैर्नियमेन वा।
मानसं वृद्धसेवाभिः सदा पार्थापकर्षसि॥९०॥
कुन्तीकुमार! क्या तुम ओषधिसेवन या पथ्य-
भोजन आदि नियमोंके पालनद्वारा अपने शारीरिक
कष्टको तथा वृद्ध पुरुषोंकी सेवाकप सत्संगद्वारा मानसिक
संतापको सदा दूर करते रहते हो?॥९०॥
कच्चिद् वैद्याश्चिकित्सायामष्टाङ्गायां विशारदाः।
सुहृदश्चानुरक्ताश्च शरीरे ते हिताः सदा॥९१॥
तुम्हारे वैद्य अष्टांगचिकित्सामें कुशल, हितैषी,
प्रेमी एवं तुम्हारे शरीरको स्वस्थ रखनेके प्रयत्नमें सदा
संलग्न रहनेवाले हैं न?॥९१॥
कच्चिन्न लोभान्मोहाद् वा मानाद् वापि विशाम्पते।
अर्थिप्रत्यर्थिनः प्राप्तान् न पश्यसि कथंचन॥९२॥
नरेश्वर! कहीं ऐसा तो नहीं होता कि तुम अपने
यहाँ आये हुए अर्थी (याचक) और प्रत्यर्थी (राजाकी
ओरसे मिली हुई वृत्ति बंद हो जानेसे दुःखी हो पुनः
उसीको पानेके लिये प्रार्थी)-की ओर लोभ, मोह
अथवा अभिमानवश किसी प्रकार आँख उठाकर
देखतेतक नहीं?॥९२॥
कच्चिन्न लोभान्मोहाद् वा विश्रम्भात् प्रणयेन वा।
आश्रितानां मनुष्याणां वृत्तिं त्वं संरुणसि वै॥९३॥
कहीं अपने आश्रितजनोंकी जीविकावृत्तिको तुम
लोभ, मोह, आत्मविश्वास अथवा आसक्तिसे बंद तो
नहीं कर देते?॥९३॥
कच्चित् पौरा न सहिता ये च ते राष्ट्रवासिनः।
त्वया सह विरुध्यन्ते परैः क्रीताः कथंचन॥९४॥
...कर राज्र करके ग्रामाधिपतिको दे, ग्रामाधिपति नगराधिपतिक...

Original Sanskrit Plate - 6

...दूर ऊपर खराद ता नहीं लिया. है ?॥ ९४॥
कच्चिन्न दुर्बल: शत्रुबलेन परिपीडित:।
मन्त्रेण बलवान् कश्चिदुभाभ्यां च कर्थचन॥ ९५॥

कोई दुर्बल शत्रु जो तुम्हारे द्वारा पहले बलपूर्वक
पीड़ित किया गया (किंतु मारा नहीं गया), अब
मन्त्रणाशक्ति अथवा मन्त्रणा और सेना दोनों ही
शक्तियोंसे किसी तरह बलवान् होकर सिर तो नहीं
उठा रहा है ?॥ ९५॥

कच्चित् सर्वेऽनुरक्तास्त्वां भूमिपालाः प्रधानतः।
कच्चित् प्राणांस्त्वदर्थेषु संत्यजन्ति लयाऽऽदृताः॥ ९६॥

क्या सभी मुख्य-मुख्य भूपाल तुमसे प्रेम रखते
हैं? क्या वे तुम्हारे द्वारा सम्मान पाकर तुम्हारे लिये
अपने प्राणोंकी बलि दे सकते हैं?॥ ९६॥

कच्चित् ते सर्वविद्यासु गुणतोऽर्चा प्रवर्तते।
ब्राह्मणानां च साधूनां तव नैःश्रेयसी शुभा।
दक्षिणास्त्वं ददास्येषां नित्यं स्वर्गापवर्गदाः॥ ९७॥

क्या तुम्हारे मनमें सभी विद्याओंके प्रति गुणके
अनुसार आदरका भाव है? क्या तुम ब्राह्मणों तथा साधु-
संतोंकी सेवा-पूजा करते हो? जो तुम्हारे लिये शुभ एवं
कल्याणकारिणी है। इन ब्राह्मणोंको तुम सदा दक्षिणा तो
देते रहते हो न? क्योंकि वह स्वर्ग और मोक्षकी प्राप्ति
करानेवाली है॥ ९७॥

कच्चिद् धर्मे त्रयीमूले पूर्वैरुचरिते जनैः।
यतमानस्तथा कर्तुं तस्मिन् कर्माणि वर्तसे॥ ९८॥

तीनों वेद ही जिसके मूल हैं और पूर्वपुरुषोंने
जिसका आचरण किया है, उस धर्मका अनुष्ठान
करनेके लिये तुम अपने पूर्वजोंकी ही भाँति प्रयत्नशील
तो रहते हो? धर्मानुकूल कर्ममें ही तुम्हारी प्रवृत्ति तो
रहती है?॥ ९८॥

कच्चित्तव गृहेऽन्नानि स्वादूद्यश्नन्ति वै द्विजाः।
गुणवन्ति गुणोपेतास्तवाध्यर्हं सदक्षिणम्॥ ९९॥

क्या तुम्हारे महलोंमें तुम्हारी आँखोंके सामने गुणवान्
ब्राह्मण स्वादिष्ट और गुणकारक अन्न भोजन करते हैं?
और भोजनके पश्चात् उन्हें दक्षिणा दो जाती है?॥ ९९॥

कच्चित् क्रतूनेकचित्तो वाजपेयांश्च सर्वशः।
पुण्डरीकांश्च कांश्चेन यतसे कर्तुमात्मवान्॥ १००॥

अपने मनको वशमें करके एकाग्रचित्त हो वाजपेय

कच्चिज्ज्ञातीन् गुरून् वृद्धान् दैवतांस्तापसान्पि।
चैत्यांश्च वृक्षान् कल्याणान् ब्राह्मणांश्च नमस्यसि॥ १०१॥

जाति-भाई, गुरुजन, वृद्ध पुरुष, देवता, तापस
चैत्यवृक्ष (पीपल) आदि तथा कल्याणकारी ब्राह्मणोंको
नमस्कार तो करते हो न?॥ १०१॥

कच्चिच्छोको न मन्युर्वा त्वया प्रोत्याद्यतेऽनघ।
अपि मङ्गलहस्तश्च जनः पार्श्वे नु तिष्ठति॥ १०२॥

निष्पाप नरेश! तुम किसीके मनमें शोक या क्रोध
तो नहीं पैदा करते? तुम्हारे पास कोई मनुष्य हाथमें
मंगलसामग्री लेकर सदा उपस्थित रहता है न?॥ १०२॥

कच्चिद्देषा च ते बुद्धिर्वृत्तिरेषा च तेऽनघ।
आयुष्या च यशस्या च धर्मकामार्थदर्शिनी॥ १०३॥

पापरहित युधिष्ठिर! अबतक जैसा बतलाया गया
है, उसके अनुसार ही तुम्हारी बुद्धि और वृत्ति (विचार
और आचार) है न? ऐसी धर्मानुकूल बुद्धि और वृत्ति
आयु तथा यशको बढ़ानेवाली एवं धर्म, अर्थ तथा
कामको पूर्ण करनेवाली है॥ १०३॥

एतया वर्तमानस्य बुद्ध्या राष्ट्रं न सीदति।
विजित्य च महीं राजा सोऽत्यन्तसुखमेधते॥ १०४॥

जो ऐसी बुद्धिके अनुसार बर्ताव करता है, उसके
राष्ट्र कभी संकटमें नहीं पड़ता। वह राजा सारी पृथ्वीको
जीतकर बड़े सुखसे दिनोंदिन उन्नति करता है?॥ १०४॥

कच्चिदार्यो विशुद्धात्मा क्षारितश्चौरकर्मणि।
अदृष्टशास्त्रकुशलैर्लोभाद् वध्यते शुचिः॥ १०५॥

कहीं ऐसा तो नहीं होता कि शास्त्रकुशल विद्वानोंके
संग न करनेवाले तुम्हारे मूर्ख मन्त्रियोंने किसो विशुद्ध
हृदयवाले श्रेष्ठ एवं पवित्र पुरुषपर चोरीका अपराध
लगाकर उसका सारा धन हड़प लिया हो? और फिर
अधिक धनके लोभसे वे उसे प्राणदण्ड देते हों?॥ १०५॥

दुष्टो गृहीतस्तत्कारी तज्ज्ञैर्दृष्टः सकारणः।
कच्चिन्न मुच्यते स्तेनो द्रव्यलोभान्नरर्षभ॥ १०६॥

नरश्रेष्ठ! कोई ऐसा दुष्ट चोर जो चोरी करते
समय गृहस्वामीद्वारा देख लिया गया और चोरीके
मालसहित पकड़ लिया गया हो, धनके लोभसे छोड़
तो नहीं दिया जाता?॥ १०६॥

उत्पन्नान् कच्चिदाढ्यस्य दरिद्रस्य च भारत।
अर्थान् च मिथ्या पश्यन्ति तवामात्या हृता धनैः॥ १०७॥

Original Sanskrit Plate - 7

Original Sanskrit Plate - 8

कच्चित् सूत्राणि सर्वाणि गृह्णासि भरतर्षभ।
हस्तिसूत्राश्वसूत्राणि रथसूत्राणि वा विभो॥१२१॥
भरतश्रेष्ठ। क्या तुम संक्षेपसे सिद्धान्तका प्रति-
पादन करनेवाले सभी सूत्रग्रन्थ—हस्तिसूत्र, अश्वसूत्र
एवं रथसूत्र आदिका संग्रह (पठन एवं अभ्यास) करते
रहते हो?॥१२१॥

कच्चिदभ्यस्यते सम्यग् गृहे ते भरतर्षभ।
धनुर्वेदस्य सूत्रं वै यन्त्रसूत्रं च नागरम्॥१२२॥
भरतकुलभूषण। क्या तुम्हारे घरपर धनुर्वेदसूत्र,
यन्त्रसूत्र और नागरिक सूत्रका अच्छी तरह अभ्यास
किया जाता है?॥१२२॥

कच्चिदस्त्राणि सर्वाणि ब्रह्मदण्डश्च तेऽनघ।
विषयोगास्तथा सर्वे विदिताः शत्रुनाशनाः॥१२३॥
निष्पाप नरेश। तुम्हें सब प्रकारके अस्त्र (जो
मन्त्रबलसे प्रयुक्त होते हैं), वेदोक्त दण्ड-विधान तथा
शत्रुओंका नाश करनेवाले सब प्रकारके विषप्रयोग ज्ञात
हैं न?॥१२३॥

कच्चिदग्निभयाच्चैव सर्व व्यालभयात् तथा।
रोगरक्षोभयाच्चैव राष्ट्रं स्वं परिरक्षसि॥१२४॥
क्या तुम अग्नि, सर्प, रोग तथा राक्षसोंके भयसे
अपने सम्पूर्ण राष्ट्रकी रक्षा करते हो?॥१२४॥

कच्चिदन्धांश्च मूकांश्च पङ्गून् व्यङ्गानबान्धवान्।
पितेव पासि धर्मज्ञ तथा प्रव्रजितानपि॥१२५॥

दिया (त्याग दिया) है?॥१२६॥

वैशम्पायन उवाच
ततः कुरूणामृषभो महात्मा
श्रुत्वा गिरो ब्राह्मणसत्तमस्य।
प्रणम्य पादावभिवाद्य तुष्टो
राजाब्रवीन्नारदं देवरूपम्॥१२७॥
वैशम्पायनजी कहते हैं—जनमेजय! कुरुश्रेष्ठ महात्मा
राजा युधिष्ठिरने ब्रह्माके पुत्रोंमें श्रेष्ठ नारदजीका वह
वचन सुनकर उनके दोनों चरणोंमें प्रणाम एवं अभिवादन
किया और अत्यन्त संतुष्ट हो देवस्वरूप नारदजीसे कहा।

युधिष्ठिर उवाच
एवं करिष्यामि यथा त्वयोक्तं
प्रजा हि मे भूय एवाभिवृद्धा।
उक्त्वा तथा चैव चकार राजा
लेभे महीं सागरमेखलां स॥१२८॥
युधिष्ठिर बोले—देवर्षे! आपने जैसा उपदेश
दिया है, वैसा ही करूँगा। आपके इस प्रवचनसे मेरी
प्रजा और भी बढ़ गयी है। ऐसा कहकर तब
युधिष्ठिरने वैसा ही आचरण किया और इसीसे
समुद्रपर्यन्त पृथ्वीका राज्य पा लिया॥१२८॥

नारद उवाच
एवं यो वर्तते राजा चातुर्वर्ण्यस्य रक्षणे।
स विहृत्येह सुसुखी शक्रस्येति सलोकताम्॥१२९॥

Original Sanskrit Plate - 9

The Checklist

Narada's instructions to Yudhishthira and to all Statesmen

1   Wellbeing of LokPal

Narada Muni begins by asking the Emperor, King Yudhishthir about his personal well being. A LokPal's personal well being is defined by the financial stability of his country. The country runs on good financial institutions which provide stability to Jana (the population that the king is serving). Without a stable financial system, a king may not be able to provide security, stability to the population. While Narada muni is speaking to the LokPal in the assembly of his brothers, great sages, graduates (स्नातक) and intelligentsia, many subordinates of LokPal are taking notes. Lokpal Yudhishthira is listening attentively. "When a student is qualified, the teacher feels respected." *Special emphasis is given to the education of LokPal* (लोकपाल). The important educational content for a LokPal are:

1. Yog (for stability of body, mind & senses)
2. Knowledge of discernment between Dharma & Adharma
3. Knowledge of all types of weapons & systems that could be made available at his command
4. Knowledge of warfare - both covert & overt
5. Games like Chess
6. Sports to develop competitiveness
7. Maintaining personal health
8. Maintaining a balanced sense-enjoyment
9. Arthashastra - the cherished book for overall development of society
10. Deep study of previous Kings mentioned in Puranas, Mahabharat, Ramayana and Vedas

11. Respect and Veneration for those teachers who impart the knowledge as mentioned above

The above education enables the LokPal to make good decisions in all situations. *The current political systems do not emphasize upon any of the above education contents which results in bad decisions as well as weakness in decision-making at critical times.* Just like a good doctor has proper education as well as experience, similarly, a good LokPal also needs a good education as well as experience. *The vote based selection process often results in money being the most important factor in selecting the LokPal.*

A LokPal needs to be qualified in all ways to properly handle his state.

- Mentally
- Physically
- Educationally
- Skill
- Competence
- Loyalty

2   Focus on Dharma

Narada muni's next question to the LokPal is "Is your mind deriving pleasure in dharma[22]?". A king is supposed to be a representative of dharma.

Dharma means compulsory code of conduct for the benefit of all. In Sanskrit Dharma also means compulsory duty, intrinsic quality, complete allegiance to Vedic literatures and actions based on vedic literatures..

If the king is not enjoying practicing dharma, then he may not be able to bring peace and prosperity, thereby happiness to all sections of society.

The codes of dharma are difficult for ordinary men to understand. Narada muni is an expert on Dharma and so is the King, so both of them understood the purpose and depth of the question.

For a Lokpal, adherence to Dharma brings spiritual and material protection from the divine.

How is Sanatana Dharma implemented in a society?

Through varnashrama, a system of four orders and four naturally existing categories of society.

Four categories are:

- Teachers
- Administrators including law enforcement
- Traders

- Artisans, Engineers, Doctors, Musicians, Artists, Actors and other specialized professions

Four Orders are:

- Spiritual renunciants
- Wandering preachers
- Families
- Students

The Lokpal ensures that all Orders and Categories are cared for in the society. Without Varnashrama, society can never be peaceful. Varnashrama automatically results in productive employment for all including children because everyone is focused on their own responsibilities. It empowers every segment of the society while giving spiritual nourishment to all. *Sanatana Dharma means "compulsory natural duties to recognize the permanent relationship between 'Atma' and 'Parmatma'." Sanatana Dharma is for every living being. Nature follows Sanatana Dharma at all times because it never moves without the will of Parmatma.*

Dharma essentially comes from the teachings of Vedas. The teachings of Vedas as explained in Puranas as well as sattology of Mahabharat & Ramayan are called Dharma by Yamduta and anything against the Vedic teachings is considered as Adharma. Yamdutas tell Vishnudutas in Bhagavat Puran 6.1.40, 'यमदूता ऊचु:, वेदप्रणिहितो धर्मो ह्यधर्मस्तद्विपर्यय: । वेदो नारायण: साक्षात्स्वयम्भूरिति शुश्रुम ॥ ४० ॥ - From Vedas comes Dharma and anything opposite of Vedas is Adharma. Vedas directly represent Narayan. This we have heard from Yamaraj.' *This clarity of differentiation between Dharma and Adharma is needed for a LokPal. Without this clarity of knowledge and thought process, a LokPal will become dependent on unqualified advisors and will often be misled. LokPal must also guide his advisors on the matters of Dharma and Adharma.* Dharma brings peace, while Adharma brings misery. *In the matters of Dharma, a committee of advisors who have deep knowledge of Mahabharat, Puranas and Ramayan, must be constituted as a 'Dharma Council' to advise LokPal. Because sometimes the application of Dharma needs knowledge of all aspects of a given situation.* Yudhishthir had a Dharma Council of more than eighty-eight thousand qualified teachers who used to advise him on a regular basis. Such councils are headed by the most senior teachers in experience as well as study. But anyone's input was considered very important.

Currently Cabinet minister positions in most states are appointed on the basis of partisan politics. *However, in Loktantra the cabinet positions are based on their lifelong training on dharma. Generally, those people are appointed who have independent views on every situation. Dharma is independent of all social opinions. Dharma focuses on what is right, rather than what is expedient. Dharma focuses on what benefits everyone in the short term keeping in view the long term perspective.*

3   Is LokPal getting enough Rest

While the LokPal is submissively hearing the question, Narada Muni[23] asks another question "Are you getting enough happiness and facilities suitable for your status?". This question is extremely important for the general population. Because a king needs proper rest and facilities to ensure that he doesn't tax or trouble the population for his wants and needs.

The LokPal takes tremendous pressure and responsibility to serve the Jana. He needs to have facilities to relax and enjoy so that he is mentally and physically fit to take on the challenges.

Not only is the LokPal supposed to perform constant meditation on Hari but he also needs to protect his consciousness from attacks & disruptions by his opponents. The LokPal needs to be aware at all times of everything happening around his kingdom. For this, LokPal needs to maintain a high degree of mental and Physical wellbeing.

The LokPal needs to be happy to properly carry out his duty to his country. *LokPal needs to make sure that he gives enough time to himself so that he always remains composed in his thoughts & actions. Yudhishthir used to do exercise regularly in the morning before he used to start his day. Exercise is the best rest for the body because it relaxes the muscles.* Exercise includes pranayama & yoga. Some of the important sources for mental rest for a LokPal are:

1. Listening to the stories from Mahabharata & Ramayana
2. Listening to the stories from Puranas
3. Listening to teachers who are proficient in Vedas
4. Listening to & Reciting Bhagavad Gita

5. Pranayama
6. Physical exercise
7. Observing Sandhya Upasana (chanting mantras at sandhya)

In addition to the above, a LokPal needs to develop a special schedule where there is sufficient time to sleep in a given twenty-four hour period. A LolPal always needs his mind and body properly rested. *Yudhishthir Maharaja had a very regulated resting period. He would rise early and take rest during the day as well as night. He also had a regulated exercise schedule. He had all the facilities for exercise specially made for his usage. Even Bhagavan Ram and Bhagavan Krishna had a regulated schedule of rest & exercise. Krishna had separate facilities for exercise similar to the concepts of private gyms today.* Most political leaders today do not get proper rest due to hectic schedules and that is one of the main reasons for bad decision-making. Narada strictly instructs Yudhishthir to maintain a proper schedule for rest.

4   Stability of Mind

His next question to LokPal "Is your mind constantly engaged in meditation on Bhagavan[24] and whether you get disturbed by constant attack & disruptions on your mind?".

A king needs to constantly think about welfare for his subjects that are technically known as Janahit (जनहित). The technical words used here are Aghat / Vikshep (आघात अथवा विक्षेप) - Enemies laying the trap for the king to commit deliberate mistakes. Narada muni deliberately stresses on the mental strength of the king. A king needs to be strong enough to not be swayed from his righteous path by his enemies.

Narada Muni being the foremost thinker and an expert in logic and reasoning is checking the mental strength of the king.

Meditation is the best exercise for a LokPal to strengthen his mind. Meditation on Hari is recommended for every LokPal.

Modern psychologists and psychiatrists have no knowledge about the mind. The most detailed information about the mind is summarized in Bhagavad Gita. *The science of 'transcending the mind' is mentioned in Patanjali Yog Sutras. There is a book by the*

similar name of mine available on Amazon. Mind is independent of the body because it is something that a person carries from last birth to current birth. It is the basis of one's personality because it carries karma of multiple births in the past. *Mind cannot be made healthy. Our thoughts are not the mind. The science of overcoming the mind is Yog. Through Yog, we control or subdue the mind. Once the mind is controlled then automatically, a person experiences freedom.*

The most important tools of building the stability of mind are:

1. Mantra
2. Yog
3. Pranayama

Yudhishthir was well trained in all of those three tools. Mantra delivers a person from the clutches of mind. Yog helps a person to transcend the mind. Pranayama automatically brings peace from the mind. *Peace is experienced by the soul when mind & intelligence are controlled. The knowledge of mind, intelligence, vritti (inclination) and soul have to be extremely clear to the LokPal to make good decisions.*

Stability of mind is also attained through the training on contentment. Most political systems of the world today do not focus on stability of mind even though they talk about it a lot. External confidence and Coherent speech does not guarantee stability of mind. *Many times it has been seen that politicians are elected on the basis of prepared speeches by motivational writers. Today the irony of society is that most politicians cannot even speak without help from aides.*

Therefore, Narada advises Yudhishthir to maintain stability of mind as a prerequisite for being an effective administrator. *Every LokPal must carefully heed to this instruction.*

5   Knowledge of Varnashrama

After checking the LokPal's mental composition, he tests on his knowledge of social structure. Vedic Scriptures recommend a system of social structure based on the qualities and work of living entities. It recognizes that all people are not born equal.

From the same parent, a different set of children can be born who are suited for different types of work. The technical categorization is known as Varna (वर्ण). Varna is never defined as per birth. Varna is defined as per the quality of individual and work of the individual.

Categories of society are defined so that a King may be able to help them grow in their choice of life and profession. Therefore a king needs to understand the division of society and make provisions for all aspects of society.

Knowledge of Varnashrama[25] helps the LokPal to provide best leadership to all classes and orders of the society.

Varnashrama is expertly implemented under the guidance of a teacher and military prowess of the LokPal.

Varnashrama is a naturally existing system in the society which is reinforced through vedic education. *The propaganda by 'casteist' western academics who neither understand the purpose of Varnashrama nor the ways to use it has misguided the world on the practicality of Varnashrama.* Varnashrama has following benefits:

1. Removes unemployment completely
2. Creates a duties or 'responsible action' based society
3. Reduces policing expenditure

4. Forces politicians to become more accountable
5. Creates a smaller government but a smarter governance
6. Automatically provides more security
7. Helps reduce defense expenditure
8. Protects environment by reducing consumerism
9. Improves individual security for a citizen
10. Promotes education
11. Increases economic output
12. Removes stress caused due to politics
13. Creates a healthy society
14. Automatically promotes spirituality based on Vedas
15. Creates a Yog friendly society
16. Increases general happiness of a citizen
17. Promotes equitable distribution of wealth for all

Varnashrama actually removes hierarchy from the society because it allows every single human to focus on enhancing their potential in their occupation. In Varnasharama, the human attains the highest level of personal excellence without worrying about competition from others. *For example, a teacher becomes self-motivated to perform to the best of his/her ability. A soldier becomes self-motivated to perform to the best of his/her ability.*

In Varnashrama, everyone's skills & knowledge counts. Since Varnashrama is based on occupational duties, it automatically creates a guild of occupation who focus exclusively on development of that profession. It automatically promotes small businesses. Large corporations usually make most of the money for their owners or shareholders. Varnasharama automatically distributes wealth while increasing a support base for the small business person. *Varnasharama automatically exists in society because it is made by nature.* However, an expert Vedic Guru is needed to assist the LokPal in implementation of Varnashrama in the society. Varnasharama is the combination of four varnas based on quality of work & activities and stages of life. Varnashrama helps every human to attain the highest perfection that can be attained in human life.

Varnasharama automatically assists the society in pleasing Hari, the most popular name of God. As stated by Suta Goswami in Bhagavat Puran, 'अतः पुम्भिर्द्विजश्रेष्ठा वर्णाश्रमविभागशः । स्वनुष्ठितस्य धर्मस्य संसिद्धिर्हरितोषणम् ॥ १३ ॥ - *The highest perfection is attained by a human in Varnasharama because of being situated in a natural state. The purpose of Varnasharama is the satisfaction of Hari.'*

6   Facilities for Varna

Narada muni's next question is important for the society "Are you magnanimous enough to provide adequate facilities and policies (guidance) as practiced by your illustrious forefathers to Brahmin[27] Varna[26] (Teachers), Vaishya[28] Varna (Tradesmen, Farmers, Cow Protectors - वाणिज्य, कृषि, गो रक्षक), Shudra[29] Varna (Experts in Medicine, Engineering, Artists, and other qualified workers) as per dharma codes mentioned in Vedas?

The LokPal needs to provide facilities of growth to all sections of society through policies, systems and processes.

Every section of society needs specialized systems and policies for their growth. Here Narada muni is checking with the LokPal whether he knows the subjects and society which he is trying to serve. A king cannot serve without Policy, Institutions and Good Intentions. Dharma provides kings with Good Intentions and a capability to create policies and systems.

Narada Muni wants to know how balanced the LokPal is. Because if a LokPal is not balanced in his focus then he may not be able to rule for the benefit of people. Janhit (जनहित) should be the principal focus for the King.

For a successful reign the LokPal needs to balance Dharma (धर्म), Wealth (धन) and Personal Enjoyment (काम) appropriately to deliver the best reign for the benefit of Jana (जन).

Facilities for Teachers

- Good classrooms
- Research Libraries
- Freedom to design curriculum

Facilities for Administrators

- Access to good teachers
- Physical Exercise facilities
- Access to researchers

Facilities for Traders

- Easy taxation laws
- Access to LokPal
- Protection from Tax authorities

Facilities for Artisans and workers

- Protection from any type of exploitation
- Free healthcare, education and food
- Easy access to Teachers

LokPal needs to put all his attention in creating suitable facilities for each Varna. The state resources are to be employed in creating facilities for professional development completely FREE for the usage of all four categories of society. The trainers also need to be provided by the state. *The legal help for protection of citizens must also be completely borne by the state on a case by case basis. During Yudhishthir Maharaja's time also, the complaints against the state were directly answered by the Head of the State. No one was above Dharma.* Most civil disputes were resolved through the Panchayat legal system while most international disputes were resolved in accordance with Dharma. Tax system was regulated in accordance with Dharma but was administered directly through the offices of LokPal. *Dharma means Vedic injunctions.*

7 The Balance

Narada Muni then asks "Are you neglecting dharma for the love of wealth? Are you ignoring wealth by focusing too much on Dharma? Are you ignoring and hurting Dharma and Wealth by focusing too much on personal enjoyment? Attachment (आसक्ति) is the only result of personal enjoyment."

Any neglect on any of the three will lead the LokPal on the path of failure. Noted here is the dharma based focus on personal enjoyment. Personal enjoyment for the LokPal cannot go outside the realm of dharma. Wealth refers to wealth earned by his Kingdom following the dharmic principles as laid out for him. Dharma refers to non-fanatic application of dharma.

Any unbalanced approach will hurt Dharma (धर्म) , Artha[30] (अर्थ) and King or LokPal (राजा) himself.

The LokPal needs to balance his priorities for the optimum good of society.

How to Balance?

- Balanced taxes
- Balanced wealth generation
- Balanced imposition of dharmic duties
- Focus on state wealth generation

The four legs of Dharma are Truthfulness (सत्य), Compassion or Kindness (करुणा), Austerity (तपस्या), 'Giving' in according to Gunas (दान). Gradually all these four qualities begin to diminish in time. *In the present age these qualities are practically extinct in human society. Only one of them is present in small quantities and that is 'Truth'.* LokPal cannot ignore the economic well-being of the state as well as its citizens. LokPal cannot even ignore the four legs of Dharma or governance. LokPal cannot be only focused on his personal enjoyment because that leads to attachment which can be misused by the enemy forces. *When a LokPal becomes too attached to personal enjoyment, then the enemy uses that attachment to destroy his country.* LokPal needs to make balanced choices so that all aspects of his personal integrity and the strength of state are maintained. *A LokPal who is not balanced is usually easily corrupted by his enemies.* If a LokPal engages too much in ritualistic aspects as mentioned in Pancharatra or other religious subjects and ignores his responsibility towards economic development, regulated sense enjoyment and state subjects, then he faces rebellion in his state. *LokPal must be 'Giving' but not so much that he empties the treasury. LokPal must create systems that ensure that everything has a check & balance.*

8 Regulated Schedule

Narada Muni is now introspecting the personal life of the LokPal further by asking this question "O the best of brave and magnanimous Kings, do you follow a disciplined schedule in your daily activities according to the three divisions of time?".

According to Shruti, a LokPal needs to perform activities as per proper divisions of time for maximum effectiveness. It is generally advised to practice personal spiritual development in the morning, perform kingly duties during the day and perform dharma based personal enjoyment in the evening. This discipline will ensure a healthy king who can ensure the success of his rule.

The Morning time is for Meditation and Spiritual priorities. The Day for work and economic activities and the night for rest and personal enjoyment.

Ideally the morning time is also for thinking about the best for one's life.

Not a single political science course in the world emphasizes upon the regulated lifestyle of a LokPal. Time is of primordial importance to LokPal in order to deliver effective governance.

The advantages of early morning time (45 minutes before sunrise and 45 minutes after sunrise) for a LokPal are:

1. Perfect time for Sandhya Meditation
2. Provides unique physical strength
3. Provides mental stability

The advantages of Sandhya meditation at noon time

1. Provides mental rest
2. Rejuvenates the body & mind
3. Brings happiness

The advantages of Sandhya meditation at evening time (45 minutes before sunset & 45 minutes after sunset) are:

1. Rejuvenates the body & mind
2. Helps in analyzing the day
3. Brings resoluteness in the mind

After the Sandhya Meditation is the time for personal enjoyment and also dinner before going to rest for the night. Best times for taking rest for a LokPal is between 10pm in the night to 4am in the morning. *Breakfast & Lunch times should also be tied to Sandhya times. Ideally, breakfast & lunch follow respective sandhya times.* Three Gunas are prominent at the conjunction of times during the day. Sattva Guna is prominent during the morning Sandhya time. Rajo Guna becomes prominent after the second sandhya time during the day. Tamo Guna becomes prominent after the third Sandhya of the day. *A Lokpal must avoid any outing in the night for personal safety unless accompanied by most trusted associates.*

9   Selecting a LokPal

Narada Muni continues "With six qualities of a LokPal and seven solutions , are you constantly checking yours and your enemies strength? Are you constantly checking on yours and your enemies fourteen officials carefully? This question checks on Yudhishthir Maharaj[31]'s focus because a focused King will bring security and success to his kingdom.

Yudhishthir was already a very qualified King and a LokPal and was destined to become the emperor of the entire world. If he was not careful in his dealings he won't be able to do justice to his role. This question was a very loaded one and at the same time required deep knowledge on the part of the king to say, Yes. King had to acknowledge this in front of his entire group of ministers, brothers, teachers, and many distinguished guests.

The six powerful qualities of a King as summarized in Shruti are :

1. Power of Explanation, Logic and Reasoning (व्याख्यान शक्ति)

2. Power of Wittiness, Intelligence (प्रगलभता शक्ति)

3. Power of Expert Arguments (तर्क कुशलता शक्ति)

4. Power of remembering History (भूतकाल की स्मृति शक्ति)

5. Power of keeping an eye for future (भविष्य पर दृष्टि शक्ति)

6. Power of Expertise in formulation of Policy (नीति निपुणता शक्ति)

A king is naturally assumed to possess the above qualities in addition to having studied Shruti and Smriti carefully under qualified teachers. Being armed with the above qualities and focus on Dharma, a King is instructed to carefully apply seven solutions to different problems that he faces. *LokPal is selected from a family who has always been at the forefront of defending that land. Then the above six qualities are tested to check his qualification. Once the candidate is found to be trustworthy and suitable, then those candidates are put to test amongst their acceptability amongst the citizens. When citizens also feel comfortable with the choice, then that candidate is elected to become the LokPal.* **This is Loktantra at work.** *This is very different from democracy where the only qualification is either racial majority or religious majority. Nowadays, due to the financial corruption carried out by various industries, money plays a bigger role in elections. Social Media and MainStream Media can easily be bought by money. Most of the image building exercise is carried by the media outlets. The voice of sanity is conspicuous by its absence.* The six qualities to test in a LokPal are mentioned above. Those are the basic tests for the suitability of a LokPal candidate.

The seven solutions to the problems that a King can apply are:

1. Vedic special prayers to different devatas (मंत्र)
2. Medicine (Ayurvedic Solutions) (औषधि)
3. Strategy (इंद्रजाल)
4. Building Bridges (साम)
5. Financial Solutions / Charity / Negotiations (दाम, दान)
6. Punishment (दंड)

7. Diplomacy (भेद)

These solutions help a king to successfully resolve any problem that he faces. Armed with 6 qualities and 7 solutions a King is advised to constantly test 14 groups of officials who manage 14 strategic assets of the Kingdom.

The fourteen strategic assets of a kingdom are as below:

1. Internal Affairs (Managing cities and Countryside)
2. Important Strategic Installations
3. Infantry assets
4. Large Military Movable assets
5. Rapid Response Military assets
6. Brave Soldiers
7. Important Officials of Important Departments such as Justice, Commerce etc
8. Inner Chambers of King's residence
9. Grain Storage
10. Census Information
11. Vedic Scriptures
12. Writers
13. Treasury
14. Information on Strength of Enemies

The fourteen groups of officials that control those strategic assets have to be completely controlled by the king. After pointing out 14 groups of officials, Narada muni asks Yudhishthir "After understanding your strengths and your enemies' strength , do you make peace with a stronger enemy to increase your wealth and treasury by performing eight essential activities?

1. Increasing Agricultural produce
2. Protecting trade
3. Building defense fortifications and protecting them
4. Constructing bridges over rivers and ravines
5. Building heavy strategic mobile platforms
6. Controlling important mines of precious metals
7. Populating uninhabited lands
8. Investing in uninhabited lands

These eight solution actions are used by political professionals for the benefit of Jana (all citizens).

The fourteen ministries or departments or secretariat must be created in every state to ensure success for a LokPal in governance. *The fourteen departments directly report to the LokPal. Each department is headed by a highly qualified teacher of that subject. Also, the head of these departments must be trusted by the LokPal.* Without a proper selection process for the department heads, the state crumbles. *Democracies are failing all over the world because they are being used by one nation to interfere in other democratic nations.*

10 Eight Actions for Prosperity

Narada Muni Inquires "Whether you analyze your enemy's strengths and if the enemy is stronger, you maintain peace with the enemy and focus on performing eight activities to increase your wealth and treasury?"

1. Krishivarnikpatho - Increasing agriculture
2. Protecting Trade
3. Durg: Creating fort and its protection
4. Setu: creating bridges and ensuring its protection
5. Kunjarbandhanam: Protecting and controlling elephants by tying them
6. Khanyakarkaradanam: developing mines for gold and Jewels and administering them
7. Shunyanam: settling people in wild provinces or uninhabited regions of country
8. Niveshanam: Investment in uninhabited regions of country

Agriculture is the single most important activity for any state. It's the only occupation that directly feeds people. LokPal needs to encourage every citizen to grow their own food. Next, is the protection of milk giving animals. The LokPal needs to completely ban killing of all milk-giving animals even after they stop giving milk out of gratitude to those animals.

Military fortifications need to be built all over the country for self protection of citizens and possible use during external attacks on the state.

State needs to build new bridges and pathways for faster connectivity between people, cities and the capital. Ease of connectivity reduces overall costs of business.

Natural resources of the state need to be responsibly exploited for the benefit of the state.

Settling responsible citizens in uninhabited regions of the country helps LokPal to bring development in all parts of the state.

Many modern academics usually say that Europe brought the concept of organized development to the world. *But the above instruction of Narada to Yudhishthir shows that organized development has been existing in human society from the beginning of creation.* Agriculture is the most important focus area for any LokPal. Agriculture feeds the population, and it is the basis for economic development. Agriculture also involves protecting dairy animals from any type of exploitation. Rearing animals for meat is not recommended because it consumes more water and also creates diseases. *All large scale epidemics in the world have found their origins in organized slaughter houses.* LokPal needs to build military fortifications all over the country to protect ordinary citizens in case of any eventuality of war. All citizens must be trained in military self-defense to create a sense of self-discipline and also prepare them to serve as reservists in the state forces. Easy connectivity from borders to every part of the state is also a must so that the country can be easily defended by state forces as well as citizens.

Trained citizens must be sent to every part of the country to ensure that every part of the country grows uniformly. The state resources must be used to station large utility vehicles & aircrafts for emergency use in every part of the country to safeguard life in cases of emergency. *This is the civilian infrastructure. Military has nothing to do in creating civilian infrastructure. Military is only for protection from external enemies. Citizen policing is a far more effective option than a state based policing system. That's why military training for civilians is recommended, especially in the current age of Kaliyuga.* Mining builds wealth because most important metals are found on earth. LokPal must try to understand the type of minerals found in the land that he controls and create new mines so that more opportunities for economic development are created.

Rare earth minerals are the latest mining focus today. But traditional minerals such as iron, bauxite, silver, gold, gems, diamonds and others have been mined from the beginning of creation. Most European academics have not given an accurate account of the history of the world because of their artificial religious bias. Unfortunately, Mahabharat which was written thousands of years ago gives an account from that period of time. Even thousands of years ago, people had better governments than anything the world has seen in the last hundred years. LokTantra has existed in human society since the Treta Yuga, when Bhagavan Ram had appeared in this world.

LokPal must encourage new investments in uninhabited parts of the country as well so that populations can be equitably spread across the nation. *In some leading democracies of the world human reservations in the most barren lands are created where access to investment is discouraged through laws. Such policies are exploitative in nature.* Narada advises Yudhishthir to spread the investments in even uninhabited parts of the country because that encourages citizens to spread in even those parts of the country. *Every island that can be safely inhabited must be converted into an attractive destination where trained citizens can safely live.* Larger populations of trained citizens create and spread wealth.

11   Seven Main Groups of Ministers

Further checking on King Yudhishthir, Narada muni asks "Are your seven main groups of ministers protected by you and they haven't joined hands with your enemies? Do rich people in your kingdom free from bad habits and do they love you unconditionally?

The seven groups of ministers are:

1. Head of strategic fortifications (दुर्गपति)
2. Prime Minister (मुख्य मंत्री)
3. Head of Dharma (धर्मराज)
4. Armed Forces Chief (सेनापति)
5. Head Priest (पुरोहित)
6. Head Astrologer (मुख्य ज्योतिषी)
7. Head of Medicine (औषधि)

Ensuring the main wealthy citizens to follow the path of virtue as explained in Vedas is considered one of the main responsibilities of a King. Citizens must be trained and also encouraged to follow Vedic[32] culture for the benefit of the King. When citizens are virtuous and King is virtuous there will be naturally strong love between them. That love is essential in building trust between the state and wealthy citizens. Narada muni wants Yudhishthir to succeed as a king and therefore gives Yudhishthir a checklist for political success.

Large Cabinets or Administration is not advised by Narada. The size of Administration should be neither too small nor too big otherwise it causes a burden to exchequer. *Earlier Narada had said about fourteen departments, and here he advises seven principal groups of Ministers or Heads of those fourteen departments.* The seven groups of ministers must monitor every single aspect of the state. LokPal must carefully check all his ministers for honesty and loyalty. *He must regularly obtain information from secret services about them and their meetings with enemies of the state.* Currently, most governments of the world do not have these seven categories of ministers. They do not have the Minister of Dharma, Minister of Jyotish and Minister of Yagya ceremonies. These seven groups of ministers are headed by a Chief Minister who becomes the single voice on behalf of these groups of ministers. LokPal himself heads the ministry of Dharma because that ensures popularity for the LokPal. *LokPal automatically is the head of Judiciary on account of being the 'Minister of Dharma'.*

All medical research and food quality checks are also directly under a dedicated 'Head of Medicine'. This ensures that all citizens are healthy and the enemy is not able to spread diseases in the state. Astronomy & Astrology is an important function of the ministers of LokPal because that helps LokPal in foretelling certain situations through the mathematical calculation of the position of stars & planets. *Most of the leaders of the world today abhor such ancient sciences because of mis-propaganda by vested interests. However, in their personal capacity they would be very much interested in understanding the upcoming nature of events. Predictive mathematical modeling ignores the impact of the position of stars & planets on land & living beings.* Strategic Fortifications or Durg are all military installations as well as local centers of governance. They must be protected by a dedicated Minister.

LokPal must remain free to control the status of Dharma in his Loktantra. *The only portfolio that the LokPal must hold is the responsibility of protection of Dharma. LokPal represents the independent & neutral position of Dharma or Law or Judiciary.*

12   Knowledge of the Enemy

A LokPal is supposed to know about all types of his population whether they be friends, enemies or not so happy people in his kingdom. Narada muni asks Yudhishthira Maharaj "Are you aware of future plans of friends, enemies and unhappy people in his kingdom? Do you consider the right time for making alliances or divisions with them as per a predefined policy?

Timing is everything in political maneuvers. Right decisions at the right time as per a predetermined policy goes a long way in achieving long term objectives and that as such is the secret behind the successful statecraft. A king may apply various techniques for gathering information about his friends, enemies and not so happy people in his kingdom. In today's world it is easier to obtain information through different means. Sometimes it is more prudent to give up certain alliances if it is not for the collective good for people. In statecraft or diplomacy there are no permanent friends or enemies. Only the interest of people matters. *LokPal makes all arrangements to understand his friends as well as enemies through his counter-intelligence forces. LokPal also keeps a tab on all dissatisfied people in his state.*

A LokPal needs to maintain current data on all friends and enemies of the state. For protecting the state, every single data point is important. Covert operations by enemies against stable & prosperous states have been carried out since time immemorial. That is nothing new. Also, the strategies of countering them have also been present in human society since time-immemorial. There is no change in either tactics or strategies. The only difference today is that the standards of morality or dharma have come down. Also, the tools & technologies have evolved to create bigger destruction in the shortest possible time. Is that progress? As Kalyug (age of quarrel & hypocrisy) progresses, people will see more hypocrisy at all levels of governments and also society in general. *In this age, tools & technology assists in degrading the standards of dharma in the society. As compassion also decreases, there will be new standards of despicable human behavior that will be seen much more than what is seen today.*

LokPal must maintain an elite counterintelligence force which will ensure that he controls the narrative that is favorable to dharma. This force must be the masters of all prevalent tools & technologies for information warfare (मायावी युद्ध) as well as other tactics of sabotage. The intelligence inputs must be checked for accuracy before acting on them because sometimes an enemy may feed such information to confuse LokPal. Based on qualified inputs an immediate action must be taken to create alliances, mount an aggression, sabotage an enemy's asset, buyout a potential adversary and even political assassination of an enemy to protect Dharma. *Timeliness is of primordial importance in all such decisions. Therefore, all information must be acted upon with alacrity. LokPal keeps his emotions secret from everyone except his Guru. The relationship between the LokPal and his Guru is the most confidential. LokPal cannot trust anyone except his Guru. The Guru of LokPal is never revealed to the public.* The state works on dharma & finance. LokPal makes all his decisions to ensure protection of Dharma and stable finances.

13   Taking Care of Middle Class

Narada muni asks "Do you have an idea on how to behave with middle class and not-so-happy people ? Do you have good counsel from people who are experienced, trustworthy elderly, pure hearted, articulate, loving and also born into noble families? Have you made such people as Ministers in your administration? Because a King's victory is based on good counsel and also the security of his good counsel only"

The Sanskrit word that Narada Muni uses here is Mantrana[33] (मंत्रणा). A King must discuss all issues with qualified advisors so that he can see all aspects of any situation. King Yudhishthir is also advised to deliberate and weigh-in personally after receiving all good counsel, which must be followed by a qualified decision. The decision must also follow a certain policy that speaks of consistency.

Good decision making is an art as well as a science. The Middle Class is the most productive category of a society. They are the workhorses of society. Their protection is the biggest priority for a LokPal to ensure the financial well-being of the country.

Dissatisfied people and political opponents should never be given any position of importance in the government. Because sometimes enmity is so deep-rooted that any amount of appeasement strengthens their opposition to the LokPal. Also, the LokPal then appears weak to the eyes of his supporters. *Dissatisfied people are easily prone to be bought by enemies. LokPal should directly speak to them and try to find the reasons for their dissatisfaction, and offer solutions to remove their afflictions. If that is not successful, then the LokPal must strictly monitor them and eventually remove them from all positions of influence. LokPal must then try to financially reward them to buy their loyalty, and if that is also not successful, then LokPal must divide them so that they do not unite. But when those dissatisfied people take help from enemies to overthrow LokPal, then LokPal must punish them severely to set a precedent for the future.*

LokPal's personal advisors must be loyal and trustworthy for generations. LokPal must make all arrangements to satisfy them with positions in government as well as military. They must not be lacking in anything in any situation. *Because if loyal friends & elderly people are not taken care of then they may also become dissatisfied and may take help from enemies. Enemies always look for such people who had the trust of LokPal in the past.* Middle-class or Shudra (who work for salary) are the most important group of people for the LokPal because they are the most productive people. LokPal must regularly interact with them and find out their needs of protection and also financial stability. They should be taxed the least and must be offered highest protection by LokPal. *Skill based educational institutes must be set up to improve the skills of the middle-class. Educational certifications as well as research must be instituted to improve innovation.* When any type of exploitation is done against them, then the LokPal must personally intervene to ensure that their interests are protected.

That is the dharma for the LokPal. LokPal reserves the right to use even death penalty for those who infringe upon the rights of middle-class. Yudhishthir Maharaja protected the middle-class or shudra with his life. That's why he was very popular amongst them.

14 Securing Confidantes from Enemy

Narada Muni continues "Are you sure that your confidante secretaries and Ministers will keep your country safe? Are you making sure that enemies have not infiltrated your confidante counsels and thereby affecting the security of your country?"

The king was advised to ensure the security of his counsels also. Because counsels and the counsel both have to be protected for the security of the country.

How to protect confidantes?

1. Never meet them in public
2. Never disclose their names to anyone
3. Even in Public, never acknowledge them

Protecting the confidential identity of confidantes is the duty of a LokPal. Narada checks on Yudhishthir to ensure that he follows an official secret policy. Every LokPal must maintain discretion to protect the interests of himself and the State.

LokPal must maintain discreteness in dealing with his confidantes as well as advisors. *Yudhishthir Maharaja used to meet his confidantes in the middle of the night to ensure the protection of their identities.* Confidantes of LokPal must be from the worker class, teachers, retired military professionals as well as friends in the enemy camp. Not only should the LokPal depend on information from confidantes in his state but also on information from enemy camps. *LokPal must rescue them from any harm should their identities be disclosed in any situation. Failure to do so will weaken the position of the LokPal. LokPal doesn't exploit anyone and pays the price for everything that he obtains from his confidantes. Failure to do so results in loss of credibility of the LokPal.* LokPal has to always evaluate the quality of information coming from a confidante. *Combining that information with the information coming from state agencies, he comes to the best conclusion. LokPal acts on that conclusion instead of depending on the information from his state agencies.* If LokPal doesn't protect his counsels and confidantes then they will leave him eventually.

15   Importance of Arthashastra

After checking Yudhishthir regarding the structure of his advisory council, Narada Muni again checks on his personal daily schedule "I have no doubt on your skills and knowledge of Arthashastra and therefore I won't ask you anything on that topic. I hope you do not fall asleep at incorrect times.

At the later part of night and before dawn, do you think about your Artha (important activities and considerations)". According to smriti, One should wake up in Brahma Muhurta (1.5 Hours before sunrise) to meditate on one's interests. This is especially advisable for a King because that gives him a quiet time to focus on priorities.

Narada Muni is changing the questions just to ensure attentiveness by the king. This question about his personal schedule seems to be out of place with his earlier questions but Narada Muni being the most intelligent sage maintains interest in his conversation. He is also checking in on the King to ensure that the King is also attentive.

The most productive times for the LokPal are between 4 hours after Sunrise and 1 Hr before Sunset.

Yudhishthir was an expert on Arthashastra. *Arthashastra was reproduced by Chanakya Muni to teach his disciple Chandragupta Maurya. Chanakya also invented modern chess. Interestingly, chess has sixty-four squares which represent the sixty four qualities of Hari. Chanakya himself claimed that he has compiled Arthashastra from different Vedas, Puranas, Upanishads, Mahabharat, Ramayan and Manusmriti texts. The knowledge of Arthashastra has been prevalent in human society from the beginning of the day of Brahma which happens to be hundreds of millions of years as per human age calculations.* LokPal must know Arthashastra in detail. Arthashastra is not just an economic treatise. It is the detailed classification of social management based on Varnashrama as well as practical implementation of Sanatana Dharma in the society. Many elements of Arthashastra are already implemented in parts in all parts of the world. However, the core of Arthashastra which is LokTantra, Varnashrama and Sanatana Dharma has been purposely kept out by ignorant political leaders of the world. Arthashastra carries severe punishment for corruption, exploitation as well as deceit. Therefore, it has been partly implemented by most governments of the world. Whoever follows Artha in more degree than others becomes the leader of the world. But they can attain more success by implementing the full Arthashastra as instructed by Narada Muni. Manu Smriti is an important constituent of Arthashastra. The propaganda against Manusmriti by corrupt politicians is due to the fear of severe punishment ordained in Manusmriti for corruption of any sorts, especially, intentions. *For more details on Arthashastra and Manusmriti, please read the authorized works in Sanskrit and other Indian languages. English translations by western authors are lost in translation itself. Even some lazy Indian authors use the European translations to produce their analysis. By the time you will be reading this, my version of simplified Arthashastra will be published.*

Yudhisthir was an expert on all important topics mentioned in Arthashastra:

1. Organization of Militaries

2. Taxation
3. Social welfare for all sections of society
4. Favorable trade policies
5. Strong implementation of Dharma or Law
6. Diplomacy
7. Protection of weaker sections of Society
8. Political strategies for defeating internal or external enemies
9. Temple Construction
10. Protection of Sanatana Dharma
11. Protection of Cows and other bovine species
12. Construction of important state infrastructure
13. Strategies of winning more territories to expand Sanatana Dharma
14. Construction of Yantras or machines for social welfare
15. Panchayat system of governance
16. Loktantra system of governance
17. Personal Sadhana (Yog & Meditation)
18. Moksha (liberation from Karma cycle) for all Citizens through gradual development in Yog

These were some of the broad categories of topics mentioned in Arthashastra. However, Arthashastra goes into much more detail on every single aspect of public & personal life. Arthashastra acts on an individual level as well as social level. Without fear of severe punishment, it is impossible to keep criminals at bay from social life. Arthashastra is very lenient for followers of Dharma or law but it has sharp teeth towards demagogues. Arthashastra, if properly implemented, ensures stable economic growth as well as morality in the society. Every state must implement Arthashatra & Manusmriti for the benefit of their society. *An association of Dharmic nations must be created to assist one another in implementation of Arthashastra in their societies.*

16   Golden Rule for Secrecy

Narada Muni continues "I hope you do not deliberate on an important matter alone or with too many people. I hope that any secret decision of yours doesn't reach your enemy. Do you ensure this doesn't happen in your rule?"

Narada Muni is trying to ascertain how many people LokPal discusses his counsel with. As per Smriti, three pairs of ears is a crowd. A secret advice remains secret in only between one to two pairs of ears. That means that most counsel should only be discussed with a maximum 1 person other than himself.

A Kingdom flourishes on good economic policies. A LokPal needs to facilitate policies for generating wealth to engage all sections of society towards nation building. Nation building is a process and it evolves every moment.

No decision by the LokPal should reach the enemy. How to protect information from getting leaked?

1. Decisions should be communicated through action
2. No announcement of intentions or plans
3. No casual discussion of decisions

The best secret is that which is never spoken or written. Therefore, Narada Muni wanted to advise Yudhishthir on the importance of secrecy of official discussions. Generally most politicians do not follow this advice in the current era. *It cannot be called 'modern' in any way because it is a relative term. But if we consider quality of life, then even hundred years ago people had better quality of life if they did not come in touch with colonialists. There were many parts of the world untouched by colonialists just a hundred years ago. But now, TV, media and social media has penetrated even those pristine neighborhoods.* Secrecy should not be just a policy, but rather, it should become a culture. LokPal must discuss his initial plans only with one person. *That person should be his Guru. LokPal must also ensure that the Guru is not discussing his plans with anyone else.* In the current world, any communication device or protocol can be leaked through various means. Therefore, LokPal must not directly use any electronic device for communication. All communication must be done in-person in a sanitized environment. His staff must ensure that those places are free from any electronic interference. *Yudhishthir Maharaja used to communicate via gestures to his most confidential associates. Bhagavan Ram used to communicate only with His brother Bhagavan Lakshman.*

LokPal must make the following arrangements to ensure that his discussions never become public news.

1. There should be no fixed place or time for such confidential discussions
2. There should not be any electronic or mechanical device in the meeting location

3. All conversations should be in a soft voice audible to either listener
4. Most conversations must be ideally done during a walk
5. All written communication should be in using cryptic words & analogies
6. All written communication must be in a handwriting that doesn't resemble LokPal's

In addition to the above steps, LokPal must also ensure that his staff respects his privacy policies at all times. *Failure to comply with his wishes must carry the strictest punishment as allowed in Dharma.*

17   Knowledge of Finance & Business

Narada Muni's next question is actually testing the financial prowess of the LokPal. "I hope you are able to quickly initiate economic policies & systems where initial investment is less but returns are higher. I hope you do not become a hindrance in those economic policies or put obstacles in the path of people who can deliver such economic systems & policies for efficient wealth creation".

A LokPal may not always be an expert on wealth creation, but he should not become an encumbrance on the path of others who can easily do that. A King is always a facilitator of everyone else because he has the power to do that. The wealth for a nation is created by cooperation between all sections of society. The actions and intentions of a King need to be understood by all. Any confusion may derail the progress of the nation.

Every LokPal must develop expertise in ArthaShastra[34], an ancient treatise on Economics and governance to promote social wellbeing. Narada gives specific advice to Yudhishthir. He asks Yudhishthir whether the returns of investments of the state are higher than the investments. *In today's world every nation of the*

world maintains higher debt than even the size of their economy. Who is financing the deficit? The answer to that question will reveal the glaring artificiality of current economic systems of the world. Most debts of all nations are owned by private corporations who have no interest in the social welfare of all citizens of individual nations.

Narada Muni is directly advising Yudhishthir to not keep any debt on the state. The state's wealth must be in the good health of citizens, good education of citizens, abundance of grains & vegetables, gold, silver, precious stones, cows, bulls and agricultural lands. *Bulls must be used in place of machines to till all agricultural lands because it helps in producing truly organic food.* When the healthcare expenses of the nation are low then automatically those funds are available for other economic purposes. A well educated citizen contributes to the economy of a nation. *The real education is the education from Ramayana & Mahabharata.*

LokPal must not interfere in the work of experts instituted by him to carry out the tasks of economic development. However, when he observes that the economic policies are not benefitting all citizens as per dharma, then he must interfere by first reprimanding his minister in charge of economic policies. Then, he must check whether his economic advisors are corrupted by enemies. If the situation doesn't change within a month, then he must appoint another qualified minister to bring back the ideal economic growth.

Any further delay than a month will result in a long term stagnation in the economy. LokPal must never give false assurances on the economy because the condition of the economy is felt in the heart of every citizen. A prolonged dissatisfaction amongst the citizens will result in revolt.

18 Protect Farmers & Workers

Narada Muni asks the LokPal "I hope that your farmers and workers are not unaware of your name, intentions, policies and expertise. Are you keeping track of their activities, needs and their work? I hope you trust them and you maintain consistency in their employment with your administration.

Because in a great endeavor or in progress like this, their loving cooperation is essential. When they know you properly, you will gain their loyalty and their love."

A King needs to take care of his subjects like he takes care of his own children. **Respect and loyalty is earned, not commanded.** A king earns respect and loyalty through his behavior and policies.

Behavior and policies go hand in hand in making King increase his popularity. Agriculture is the most essential part of the security of a nation. A nation that cannot produce its own food is vulnerable to its enemies. After all, everyone needs food. Food security is an essential part of a nation's security apparatus. It drives all other economic and nation building processes.

The LokPal needs to ensure that workers and farmers know his plans, actions and intentions. When citizens clearly understand the intentions of LokPal, then they may even forgive the apparent lack of good performance of most economic indicators. *But when the intentions are suspect, then it will result in a revolt against the LokPal.* **Workers & Farmers are the most important constituents for a LokPal because it is the largest**

population segment of any society. *The Sanskrit word Shudra means a salaried class of workers. It doesn't mean a lower caste. Doctors, Engineers and any other profession that works on salaries falls into that category. They are the most productive of all Varnas because they actually make the society prosper economically.*

A LokPal can implement the instructions of Narada by doing the following.

1. Set up a separate department to focus on existing professions and also create new ones based on new emerging professions
2. Get the best experts to train workforces Free of charge to the trainee
3. Develop certification & license systems to ensure quality
4. Monitor corruption and take decisive punitive actions against those who interfere in the freedom of workers & farmers
5. Provide state assistance to farmers who need such help with conditions on their performance
6. All lands are officially owned by the state and LokPal must make agreements to give those lands to farmers on a rotation basis of 2 years.
7. Create simple systems for buying of produce from workers & farmers
8. Create simple systems for payment to farmers & workers at prices that must be announced at least one month in advance.
9. Create simple taxation system for farmers & workers

LokPal may make additional programs of giving donations to needy workers & farmers based on their economic conditions. LokPal must ensure that no worker or farmer sleeps hungry in his state. *LokPal must also create checks & balances which dissuade the worker & farmer to take undue advantage of the friendly policies of LokPal.* The punishment for promoting corruption that works against the interests of farmers & workers are:

1. Death punishment
2. Lifetime imprisonment
3. Menial service to the society without any remuneration other than food and public shelter

These punishments dissuade corruption conclusively. Due to the fear of punishment, the corruption gets completely rooted out in the state of LokPal. When farmers & workers are protected then prosperity reigns for everyone else in the society.

19   Art of Delegation

Therefore Narada Muni asks Yudhishthir "I hope that you have delegated important activities like Agriculture to your trusted and honest workers who have served your family for generations."

Also, stability of employment is important to workers. Stable employment makes workers stable and more productive to the state. That's what Narada Muni is testing King Yudhishthir on.

Agriculture cannot be left to anyone but the most trusted family member or any other person who's loyalty to LokPal is beyond any doubt. That's why, importance is given to agriculture by Narada muni. Farmer's interest should be paramount in the kingdom because that is the only section of society that focuses on food production.

A LokPal needs to focus on results. Because results speak louder than intentions and words. *In the case of the Pandavas, the responsibility of agriculture was given directly to Sahadeva, the youngest brother of Yudhishthir Maharaja.* Agriculture must be organic in nature because that ensures natural rejuvenation of soil. *Food production must be as per the local characteristics of the soil. Globalization has led to international food tastes which may require additional resources to grow food.*

Importance of Agriculture to LokPal

1. Food Security
2. Seed security
3. Independence of State

The Department of Agriculture should not be left to untrustworthy ministers who have a previous record of corruption. *Agriculture is the single biggest priority for LokPal. Agriculture feeds the society. Other trade & commerce run on the basis of secure food supply. When a country doesn't have enough food to feed its population then it becomes weak because the enemies exploit food shortages to extract favorable trade deals.* Further checks & balances on the qualifications and performance of even close relatives must be maintained so that nepotism is not allowed to fester.

20   Focus on action, not Rhetoric

Narada Muni inquires "I hope that you announce your actions & policies after they are successful or near success. I hope that you ensure that people know about your actions after they are successfully completed. Do you get your important work such as Agriculture done by trustworthy, loyal and elderly people who have been serving your family for centuries?

Do you ensure this happens?" This question is so pertinent in today's Information Age. There is a general tendency to earn brownie points before any action. Narada Muni strictly advises against such efforts. When a king focuses on action more than rhetoric, he earns the trust of his subjects.

For a king to rule efficiently, he needs to ensure that the population needs to be educated. A king needs to maintain an education system to produce a well educated population. LokPal must announce only successful outcomes. *When a LokPal announces intentions without actual successful implementations then LokPal loses popularity with the masses. Due to pressures of media*

and politics, some politicians announce their intentions prematurely which actually harms their credibility in the long term. It is also important to educate the public about the programs which have been successfully implemented. When LokPal announces a successful outcome, he gains prestige in the eyes of the public. *LokPal must also publicly announce his failures and reasons for those failures. Such acceptance of failures enhances trust in the public.* LokPal must always maintain an emotional connection with the public in general. *When a LokPal publicly displays his strengths and vulnerability in public, then the public becomes emotionally connected with that LokPal.*

21   Ensuring Quality of Teachers

Narada muni then asks "Are your teachers well educated in all Vedic Shastra and also dharma ? Are your teachers well equipped to impart relevant training to your Princes, Important officials and Principal warriors?

The word relevant training and education is important. Every state needs to decide their own curriculum for the benefit of the state. Here Narada Muni emphasizes specialized education for princes, warriors and important officials in addition to education for the general masses. The university system was a very active department of the LokPal. Also, the qualification of teachers was based on merit.

An educated LokPal automatically attracts intelligentsia. The family of LokPal must also be very well educated within the country. A foreign educated LokPal cannot connect with his citizens. Therefore, a LokPal must be educated in line with Vedic knowledge.

A LokPal

- Must be educated in his country's premier education that focuses on Vedic knowledge
- His family must be also educated within the countries' premier education institutions that deliver Vedic education
- Must be able to distinguish between Dharma and Adharma
- Must be able to take clear decisions in line with Dharma

Dharma is the principal theme of Vedas. Dharma represents the ideal standard that is followed by everyone and everything at all times. Dharma means essential quality, intrinsic quality, law and denotes the essence of everything. The meaning of Dharma is defined in Vedas and all histories connected with Vedic truths. *'Anything and Everything as per Vedas is dharma and anything opposite of Vedas is Adharma.'* Any teacher who has not studied from Vedas cannot be qualified to teach anyone else. *Women were given the same training on dharma as men because they are responsible for bringing up qualified children. Pandavas' mother Kunti was trained in all departments of Vedic knowledge.* Every citizen of any land must be trained in Vedic knowledge. The best place to start is to teach Bhagavad Gita to every citizen of the world irrespective of their location. *The quality of teachers determine the quality of students.*

The principal quality of a teacher for LokPal are

1. Must have served his teacher humbly & submissively
2. Must have studied Vedic knowledge under a guidance for at least 15 years of his youth & adolescent life
3. Must have travelled all over the country to connect directly with people
4. Must have done menial service to his Guru
5. Must have been a good student himself
6. Must have complete control over his mind & senses
7. Must have been a lifelong practitioner of Yog
8. Must have been trained in warfare and war strategies

Without qualified teachers it is not possible to train a LokPal for the future. Ideally, the LokPal is also a Yogi because that makes him qualified to administer Dharma. *LokPal actually administers Dharma to his citizens.* Therefore, Narada asks Yudhishthir whether his teachers are trained in Vedas and whether they impart relevant training to his princes, important officials and warriors. Without martial training, a LokPal doesn't become qualified to hold an office. *All pandavas were trained in advanced warfare by Dronacharya. Bhagavan Ram was trained in advanced weaponry by Vishvamitra.*

22   Award Meritocracy in Education

Narada Muni wanted to ensure from the LokPal "I hope that you select an intelligent scholar from amongst thousands of such scholars. Do you respectfully accept the most intelligent of all scholars? Because an intelligent person can deliver you from the worst economic problem and perform a greater task for you?"

Here the importance is given to merit. Only meritorious people can add value to a king. For a king, the best professional is needed. Only the most meritorious of all matter for a king to be his counsel.

Narada Muni wants to verify whether LokPal is careful in selecting his counsel "I hope you respectfully hire the services of one learned man out of thousands of fools. Because a learned and intelligent person can save you from the most debilitating economic problem".

After checking in on the King about his selection process, Narada muni wants to understand from the King about his security preparedness. The Sanskrit word durg (दुर्ग) represents an important strategic fortification of the King and may include palaces, military installations, hospitals and any other place of strategic importance to the kingdom.

The LokPal must always prepare his armies for war at all times. A well prepared army ensures the protection of the state as well as LokPal. The state must make all provisions to improve the standards of education for its citizens. It is the principal duty of a LokPal to train all his citizens in all departments of Vedas based on their inclination. The ideal system of education is the vedic education as imparted in Gurukuls. All teachers must be trained in all aspects of Vedic education such as Dharma, Logic & Reasoning, Sankhya (science, geography, world knowledge) and mathematics. Depending on their inclination, teachers may be additionally trained in topics of their interests. Then, such qualified teachers who have been certified by their respective Gurus must be employed by LokPal to teach citizens all over the state.

No teacher must have more than 25 students in each class because anything more than that is unmanageable for a teacher. The teacher must not only give theoretical training to their students but also engage them in direct service to his school through various projects. *This creates a close working relationship between the teachers and their students.* Over the period of close observance of students, the teacher will be able to recommend the future advanced training for his students. Based on inclination & interest, various students are put into professional training for further acceptance into various professions. *The current western model of education is untenable because it is only designed for employment purposes of western economy. That model is unsuitable for the rest of the world. But the education system mentioned here is tenable for every part of the world.*

The recommended training program for citizens:

1. From 5-14 age groups - Basic education on Dharma, Sankhya, Logic & Reasoning, Astrology, and Vedic Mathematics

2. From age group 14 onwards - Specialized education in Skills, warfare, administration, and politics as per Dharma

LokPal must maintain all education free for students and should be ready to employ all qualified students as well as new teachers at all times. Ten percent of all tax collections must be spent on the education of citizens. Qualified teachers must be selected to advise LokPal on the education policy of his state. Then, those teachers must also be used for teaching and preparing the next batch of leaders for the state. *The importance of qualified counsel to the LokPal is emphasized herein. LokPal must receive the best counsel at all times so that he can make best decisions for the protection of his citizens.* **Teachers must always be paid on time to avoid corruption in education.**

The awards for teachers must be given directly by the LokPal:

1. Awards for 20 years of service to society
2. Awards for excellence in specific topics

23   Ensure Abundance of Resources

Narada Muni then inquires "Are your fortifications filled with wealth, automatic weapons, hand held weapons, water, food, machine based weapons, engineers, and trained soldiers?" A Lokpal needs to ensure that all his strategic assets are well protected. King cannot take any chances whatsoever.

A LokPal needs to maintain

- Best armies
- Abundant storage of grains and essential supplies for long term war
- Quality drinking water
- Machine based warfare tools
- Engineers
- Medical supplies for armies
- Best possible training for the armies

The LokPal must ensure that his armies and logistics are always ready to wage a three year full-blown war at all times. Ensuring abundance of supplies at all times can be easily attained by ensuring a six month rotation of rations for the state. *Every six months, the old stock must be released after the equal amount has been deposited. This requires very strong warehouse management.* Ponds must be created all over the state for water storage as well as water harvesting. Natural plant based remedies for all types of ailments must be taught to each citizen to ensure good preventative health. Every LokPal must make plans to modernize the armed forces to take care of all immediate and long term defense needs. *Such actions increase the popularity of LokPal.* Engineering as a profession has always existed in human society. Every locale of earth produces engineers and they must be employed by LokPal to create unique indigenous marvels such as buildings, bridges and dams. *LokPal must not only employ such engineers but also provide them with all state funded projects to hone their skills.* Promoting engineering also helps in increasing the trust of the citizens.

The state that prepares for war, doesn't face defeat in the war. LokPal must train all citizens in warfare but employ the best amongst them for the standing armies. In the case of emergency all citizens can be employed to defend the land if such need arises. All citizens must be trained in basic defense, basic offense and also covert operations. A separate citizens volunteer force must also be constituted to maintain internal security. *Organizations are created only for training and management. But loyalty to the state drives performance in internal security. Police are not recommended because it is a colonial concept. Also police creates an additional layer between the state and citizens. Every citizen must be trusted to police their neighborhoods and bring lawbreakers to the justice department headed by the LokPal.*

Armies must also hold regular training with only those friendly states who are willing to use their forces to defend alongside LokPal's armies. Armies must be trained to use their powers to defend lakes, ponds and rivers from pollution as well as possible poisoning by the enemies. *Standing Armies must always be kept away from common citizens because that destroys their orientation. Armies must be trained to inflict maximum damage to enemies. At any given point of time the size of the standing army must be 10% of the total population of the state. The armies must be maintained using 20% of state taxes.* A LokPal that creates abundance in the state remains popular at all times.

24 Focus on Quality of Minister

Narada muni informs LokPal "Even one Minister who is intelligent, brave, courageous, and capable can deliver large assets and wealth to the King."

The qualification of a Secretary or Minister is extremely important. Secretary or Minister must be

- Well educated
- Experienced
- Loyal

In addition all ministers must be born within the state and must be also educated within the state. Ministers must be trained to execute their duties in the most professional & exemplary manner. Any failure on delivery by a minister reflects on the competency of the LokPal. Every minister must be tasked with specific responsibilities and goals for every year. Failure to attain those goals must be punished with either demotion or removal from that position. LokPal must not hesitate to make his intentions very clear with every minister that he appoints to manage his departments. All ministers must be paid very good salaries to perform their duties to the state. In case of exceptional delivery of outcomes, LokPal must award his ministers with additional title and responsibility to set an example for others. LokPal must choose the very best from the state to take responsibilities of a minister.

All ministers must be tasked to obtain a new asset or create additional wealth for the state. Failure to do so must be a criterion for disqualification in the succeeding year. All goals must be set for a year with a vision for twenty years. *LokPal must never disclose his secret plans to all his ministers. Those plans must only be discussed with his Guru. The loyalty of ministers must always be tested by the secret service of the LokPal.* All ministers must be ready to fight in the war should the need arise. Ministers must be allotted portfolios based on their experience of delivery at a lower state position. *Generally, kings of districts within the country were appointed as ministers for the LokPal.*

25   Eighteen Strategic points of Interest

Narada muni points out the places where the King needs to focus to ensure security to himself and his State. "I hope you keep track and take good care of your eighteen enemies and your fifteen important strategic points of interest (POI) through at least three spies for each strategic POI."

The eighteen Strategic Points of Interest of enemies as pointed out by Narada muni are:

1. Ministers / Officials
2. Priests
3. Prince or Heir to the Kingdom
4. Head of Armed Forces
5. Doorkeepers
6. Head of inner chambers of the Palace
7. Head of the Prison system
8. Head of Treasury
9. Secretaries responsible for spending state money
10. Guard Manager
11. Chief of cities
12. Manager of State Engineers
13. Head of Religious system
14. Speaker of the State Assembly
15. Head of Judiciary
16. Head of King's palace
17. Head of Border security forces
18. Head of Forest Management

There needs to be a department for At Least 54 specialized spies and a department to track activities of all important officials. Any state needs to have these departments to ensure the smooth functioning of the state. *LokPal must not be lenient with punishment for disloyalty to the state as per Dharma. Any dereliction of duties must be treated on par with disloyalty to the state. Fear of punishment drives performance for the state. When the ministers or important officials are left uncontrolled then they loot the state thereby resulting in revolt by the citizens against the LokPal.* Ministers & Officials must be made aware of the severe consequences of dereliction of their duties towards the state. *It is easy for enemies to infiltrate LokPal's defenses through foreign religious organizations. LokPal must regulate all foreign religious instructions to follow the Dharma of the land. Failure to comply must be punished through proactive covert actions against the enemy states from where they receive their motivation. In case such actions do not yield results, then the LokPal must be willing to engage in a direct military confrontation with those states.* Any foreign intervention in any of the eighteen important departments of the state must result in capital punishment for the officials angaging in such corruption. *In addition, the foreign states must be made fully aware of the real possibility of a military confrontation.* LokPal must identify such enemy states and keep his forces near their borders should the need arise to extract peace for his state.

26   Importance of Intelligence Team

Narada inquires "The latter 15 of your own must be examined regularly." "I hope you remain unknown to your enemies, always alert and always endeavoring to keep track of all activities of your enemies." It's essential for a LokPal to maintain a spy craft to maintain tight control over his empire. LokPal must protect himself as well as protect the state apparatus.

Priests have a very important role to play in the success of a King. Priests invoke divine blessings and guide him through scriptural knowledge. Vedic scriptures contain historical examples of past successful kings who regularly take spiritual advice. *Priesthood must be protected from infiltration by enemy states. A priest who is misrepresenting Dharma as stated in Vedas, Puranas and Itihasas must be immediately put into surveillance and if found guilty must be barred to practice priesthood. Such decisions must be taken in consultations with other priests who enjoy the trust of the LokPal.* The well-being of priests who follow Dharma based on Vedas is the direct responsibility of the LokPal. *The LokPal who ignores the followers of Dharma, loses everything eventually.*

Expert management of State happens when there is a strong system of human intelligence (HUMINT). The feelings and aspirations of individuals at key places need to be known to the LokPal at all times.

HUMINT must include

- Feelings and Behavior

- Aspirations
- Ambitions
- Likes and Dislikes
- Sources of Income
- Expenditures

The secret service of LokPal must monitor every small instance of behavior of his fifteen closest officials. *That also means that the cabinet size of a LokPal must not be more than fifteen. Those fifteen officials manage eighteen departments. It is not possible to have more than eighteen departments in any given state. All other departments can be subsidiary to these eighteen major categories.* LokPal depends upon citizens to ensure compliance by his appointed officials also. Any citizen complaint must be immediately investigated for veracity. *In case of faulty complaints, the citizen must not be punished for reporting for at least ten such occurrences. If the complaints persist then the citizen must be brought for questioning by the judicial department while the official is kept under suspension until the investigation is completed. In case the citizen is found guilty, then the citizen must be barred from employment in all state departments. However, in case the official is found guilty then the official must be punished through various methods for irregularities.* The secret service holds an important responsibility in the state for LokPal. Their inputs are considered important for the delivery of outcomes to the citizens of the state. LokPal must never ignore their inputs. *Every member of the secret service must also be controlled by the secret officials of the LokPal whose identity must never be disclosed.*

27 Ensure Quality of Religious Leaders

Narada Muni wants to ensure through his question "Are your priests humble, well mannered, cultured, well-versed in multiple scriptures, intelligent, free from fault-finding and expertise in scriptural debates? Do you respect them completely?"

Teachers have to be trained not only in the technical aspect of education but also the behavioral aspect. Good Teachers are emphasized by Narada to be the pillars of society and they have to be trained well. A teacher's expertise is evaluated by his/her ability to explain complex matters in the simplest possible way. Teachers build the state. *Teachers are judged based on their knowledge of Dharma as per Vedas. Such teachers must be kept maintained personally by the LokPal.* This was the major reason why Narada wants to ensure that Yudhishthir respects teachers. Teachers are the bedrock for a successful state. Any state that ignores teachers fails in due course of time. *Teachers must be qualified in Vedic knowledge to be even considered a teacher. Teaching is a responsibility, not a profession. Currently, the world considers teaching as a profession and that is the failure of human society today. Teachers must have a strong inclination in studying Mahabharat, Ramayan and all Puranas.*

A king needs all help from intelligent people in his kingdom. He needs to follow a system that inspires his core supporters and keeps them engaged in his administration. Rituals have deep scientific meanings behind it and they invoke special blessings for the King. Vedic rituals are themselves a science. Yog is a science. Sankhya is a science. These are the sciences because they are built on Sankhya. *Teachers must be Yogi because that helps them in controlling their mind.* The principal qualities of a teacher are: Vedic Knowledge and Humility.

Vedic priests are considered the best priests for expert advice on all matters including politics. Every LokPal must employ them for political advice. *Expert scholars of Mahabharat & Ramayana are very competent in advising a LokPal on all topics connected with Dharma, Politics, Warfare and Economic Development.* Debates are a healthy way to test the knowledge of priests. *The Sanskrit word for debates is Shastrarth (शास्त्रार्थ) which means a meaningful discussion with points and counterpoints on a specific topic for the benefits of all (listeners, speakers and self).* A fault-finding priest is not helpful for a LokPal because that priest's knowledge is relative to the knowledge of another priest. Yog helps a priest develop more logical intelligence because it helps the priest overcome mind.

28   Timing is everything

Narada inquires "Have you appointed Vedic[4] Ritualistic experts, intelligent and simple teachers for your ritualistic (agnihotra) procedures? Do they provide you timely advice on what they have done and what they will be doing?".

Timing is everything in ritualistic procedures as they follow astrological[5] sequence in accordance with astrological charts of the LokPal and also of the state. Like individuals, even Land and State have proper Vastu[7] calculations.

According to Shruti[8], it is said that a King takes 1/6th of Karma[9] of the population that he is managing. He needs all the help from divine powers to get the necessary strength to discharge his obligatory and necessary duties. Expertise in ritualistic ceremonies is one of the principal qualities of teachers who have chosen that profession.

It is important for a LokPal to know as much information beforehand to make proper decisions. Health is an important area for the king. LokPal needs to ensure his personal health as well as the health of his subjects. The Health department is under the direct control of the LokPal. Ritualistic Vedic ceremonies create enthusiasm & confidence in the citizens as well as LokPal. These ceremonies allow the LokPal to communicate with citizens more personally. Also, it brings the culture of implementation of policies with mathematical precision. *Vedic culture is the most scientific culture on the planet. It is based on mathematics and therefore guarantees results. Every mantra has a meter in which it is chanted. This meter is so specific that it guarantees the outcome for which the mantra is chanted.* LokPal depends on qualified Vedic experts for timely advice on future & current events. *LokPal must weigh every single advice and make a timely decision. If decisions are not timely made then that results in collapse of the government of LokPal.* Since human lifespan is limited, the decisions have to reflect positively in the daily life of citizens.

29 Health depends on various factors

Narada inquires "Have you appointed health experts who can foresee health issues of you as well as your subjects? Do you have experts who understand planetary movements, astrological impact on earthly events, outcome of favorable / unfavorable astrological changes? Are your advisors fully capable of understanding divine influence, impact on general population and health issues using astrological calculations? Do you cross-verify the findings with a large group of experts?".

A king needs to use all facilities available at his command to preemptively predict and prepare himself with solutions for all types of eventuality. A king cannot leave things to chance. He needs to proactively make informed decisions. The health of citizens directly contributes to the overall health of the state. Every LokPal must keep basic healthcare free for all citizens. *Good healthcare is a human right, not a privilege. Healthcare must be continuously improved in relation to the change in lifestyle.* LokPal must encourage preventative health by promoting Yog, sports and also healthy vegetarian eating habits. LokPal must construct state funded facilities for sports & exercise for every citizen. That automatically ensures good health for the majority of citizens. *LokPal must regulate private profit making organizations in their research & development of new medicinal drugs. Because, there is a risk of those private organizations being also involved in creating new types of diseases. LokPal must also control his officials and ministers in dealing very closely with those private organizations.*

Allocation of work to right candidates is extremely critical for successful outcomes. Qualification of candidates usually drives the category of allocated work. The division of labor is strictly advised based on qualifications, qualities, competence and loyalty. Ayurveda (knowledge of increasing lifespan) experts automatically understand the influence of stars & planets on the general health of citizens. Such experts must be consulted regularly to plan for immediate and long term health of citizens. *LokPal is like a caring father, and it is the duty of LokPal to plan for medical contingencies arising out of natural calamities.* Astrology & Ayurveda help LokPal in planning in advance for such natural calamities. LokPal must constitute a committee of such experts in regularly advising him to plan his outcomes. Astrology is not an occult science because it is based on mathematics. *Moon & Sun have a natural strong influence on the mass behavior of the population of humans, plants and animals. Similarly other planets such as Mars, Venus, Jupiter and Saturn also have strong influence on the health & behavior of a large section of a population.*

Understanding such astrological occurrences can make a difference in the collective health of the majority of people. LokPal must take these factors into calculation before planning for the collective health of his citizens.

30 Competence should be rewarded

Narada inquires "Have you given important work to your best people according to their competence? Have you allocated medium important work to your employees according to their competence? Have you allocated not so important work to your employees according to their competence? Have you engaged them properly?"

Proper division of work ensures a favorable outcome and also employee satisfaction. *Clear allocation of responsibilities helps in getting clear outcomes. Yudhishthir Maharaja was an expert in division of labor and arrangement of large armies. He was also an expert on Arthashastra which creates a very productive society. With this knowledge, Yudhishthir was able to bring prosperity to all his citizens.* The work must be allocated based on expertise, qualification and past outcomes. How the work must be allocated to ministers & officials?

1. All work must be allocated to the head of department
2. Most important outcomes must be allotted to personal favorites (as per competence) of the LokPal
3. Head of Department must further divide the work to assistants
4. Daily progress of work must be provided to LokPal in the morning

Failure to deliver measured outcomes and reasons for not achieving outcomes must be given to LokPal in the morning. *Morning is the best time for LokPal to plan for outcomes for the benefit of his citizens. It is the duty of a LokPal to engage his ministers & officials in the most productive way. LokPal must never allot work to anyone however competent who is not loyal to him. Trust in a disloyal minister & official will result in failure for the LokPal.*

Competence of an employee is judged according to outcomes. A king needs to ensure that everyone feels satisfied with their work and everyone knows what they are supposed to do. It is said that a satisfied worker produces great results for the master. The important work needs to be entrusted with loyal and well qualified people.

The LokPal must grade his Secretaries and Ministers on two parameters:

1. Competence, and
2. Loyalty

Both parameters should be weighted 50:50 and must be given equal importance. *Without competence, outcomes will never be attained. With loyalty, outcomes will be contrary to the expectations.* In any case, LokPal must hold even the most loyal ministers & officials accountable. Without accountability, LokPal becomes ineffective.

31   Loyalty should be rewarded

Narada inquires "Do you employ non-covetous, loyal (from generations), your well-wishing and pure-hearted Ministers in the best type of work in your state?". The quality of work must meet the quality of the individual. Work motivates people.

What kind of ministers should the King look for?

- Ministers who are free from greed, covetousness and any evil designs
- Ministers whose ancestors have faithfully served the King for generations
- Ministers impeccable behavior, thoughts and character

These types of ministers must be given the best quality of work as per their qualification. It is important for a king to keep them occupied in the roles that they prefer. Keeping these types of ministers engaged in the best quality of work ensures their continued performance and best results for the king.

"Punishment is the solution for anarchy as stated in Bhagavad Gita".

However a punishment has to be commensurate with the quantum and severity of crime. If punishment goes overboard people rebel. Dissatisfied people are the biggest source of mental anxiety to the king. *LokPal must carefully consider implementing Varnashrama based on Manusmriti to create satisfied & employed citizenry. In the current age, Manusmriti can be modified to include today's expectations while not deviating from the ultimate purpose of Varnashrama which is 'pleasing Hari'.*

King's popularity depends on the efficiency of his judicial system. In fact the strength of a state is known by the strength of its judicial system. Ensuring justice to all was considered the primal responsibility of the kingdom. *Yudhishthir Maharaja was loved by all because he delivered justice to every citizen at all times. Bhagavan Ram and His father Dashrath were popular with masses because of their continuous delivery of the outcome of justice to their citizens.*

Loyalty must be rewarded

1. Financially, and
2. Through position of Honor

Both factors are equally important. *Loyalty can always be purchased by an enemy state.* LokPal must not take the loyalty of his close ministers as well as officials for granted. Loyalty must always be nurtured through words as well as physical rewards. The personal character of LokPal plays the most important role in eliciting loyalty. When a LokPal loses moral character, then it is natural for loyal ministers & officials to lose trust. *LokPal must never allow loyal ministers & officials to see his personal life. It creates an invisible barrier which gains the trust of loyal ministers & officials.*

When a LokPal engages in sense enjoyment beyond the permission of Dharma, then that LokPal loses his reputation in front of loyal ministers & officials. LokPal must always maintain balanced enjoyment, religiosity and military leadership in front of his ministers & officials. Any type of excessiveness in any sphere of interaction may result in LokPal losing the trust of his ministers.

32 Weighted Justice

Narada inquires "Whether your justice system doesn't give tough punishment to ordinary citizens thereby putting them in deep mental pain. I hope your ministers and officials govern your territory in a lawful way."

According to Narada, punishment has to be commensurate with the degree of offense. King needs to ensure that his citizens do not receive any punishment that they do not deserve. Not everyone deserves the same punishment. Punishment should be commensurate with the degree of offense, category of person and motive of offense.

The grades of punishment are:

1. Brahmanas are punished through verbal admonishment
2. Kshatriyas are punished through taking away their land
3. Vaishya are punished through financial taxes
4. Shudra are punished through physical punishment only in some special circumstances

In Kaliyuga everyone is a Shudra, and therefore, everyone is liable to punishment through physical punishment which means incarceration. *Every Yuga has different standards based on the general qualities of mass population. LokPal must ensure that no one escapes the legal judicial system of the state. Military can be used against even citizens who may be revolting against Dharma on the instigation of enemies of the state. Foreign nationals must be treated on par with citizens as long as they are within the boundaries of the state of LokPal.*

All three factors need to be weighed equally. Amongst all offenses, disloyalty to the state is considered the worst. The worst punishment should be reserved for offenses against the state. Punishment of death is recommended for traitors who sell the country's secrets to enemies or who try to assassinate the LokPal. *LokPal must always protect civilian citizens from his own ministers & officials through the strong judicial system. Since the Judiciary is directly under the control of LokPal, LokPal must make laws based on the laws of the land in accordance with the ancient history of the land. The laws of foreign cultures must be studied but never implemented.*

For all other offenses, other powers must be delegated as per Vedic knowledge systems as mentioned in Mahabharat, Puranas and Ramayan. For soldiers special tribunals must be created to adjudicate their grievances. For all professions such as medicines, engineering, trade, commerce, justices and others special laws must be created to govern them. *Barring basic rights such as Freedom of Speech, respect for every living being and loyalty to the state - all other laws must be specific to professions.* Only the actions must become the basis of administering justice. *Freedom of thought and words must be punished only when those work against the interests of the state.*

33 Controlled Taxation

Narada continues "Just like pure-hearted priests leave sinful hosts and pure-hearted women leave lusty men, similarly the subjects disrespect a King who extracts excessive taxes strictly. I hope you do not tax your subjects similarly."

It is generally assumed that sane advice cannot be given to a cruel person. Here Narada is instructing that the King doesn't tax his subjects excessively. *Unreasonable taxes gradually destroy a state. The state which taxes heavily because of its location or other natural advantages or due to any other reason fails to exist in future because its citizens will abandon it. LokPal must never tax his citizens heavily for any reason.* Taxes are extracted for only two purposes:

1. Defense of the State
2. Providing better facilities (roads, bridges, drinking water, clean environment, healthcare and security) to the citizens

Excessive taxation makes the subjects very disrespectful to the King. King needs to ensure that tax laws are humanely applied to everyone. *LokPal is considered cruel if he extracts too much taxes from his citizens. Citizens gradually disrespect that LokPal.*

Maximum tax recommended is 25% after all basic needs of an individual are met. Ordinary citizens need to be protected from excessive taxation by the state. It is LokPal's responsibility to ensure that ordinary citizens don't pay excessive taxes. *Warriors should not be taxed at all during their active service. Businessmen should be taxed at a fixed rate of 25% of their net profits. Priests & Teachers should not be taxed at all. Scientists & Engineers should not be taxed more than 25% of their net income after expenditures are deducted. Farms that own cows & bulls should not be taxed at all. Those who sell meat for profit should be taxed at 80% of their gross income. Private corporations should not be allowed to manufacture or sell any weapons. The entire weapons industry must be directly under the complete ownership and control of the LokPal.*

Farmers must be taxed only when the harvest is good. When the harvest is bad, Farmers must be given state help. Protection of farmers is a direct responsibility of LokPal. Their prosperity creates a prosperous state. LokPal must never hurt their interests. All farmers must be given free education, free access to state resources and free healthcare funded by the state. *By protecting farmers, LokPal gains trust of the state.*

Foreign traders must be taxed the same level as traders from one's own country. Foreign traders must comply with the Dharma of the state. *Failure to do so must result in expulsion of the foreign traders from the state. LokPal must enter into international trade commitments only if that protects local manufacturers & traders. All international trade deals must be approved by the respective trade regulatory bodies within the state. All imports must be equal to or less than the exports in the same category. LokPal must never accept a foreign currency within his state. International trade must be done with only those friendly states who believe in collective prosperity. Ideally, LokPal must never agree or become part of any multi-state agency to protect the interests of its own citizens.* LokPal must maintain an active military deployment near all enemy states who are near the trade routes. LokPal must be willing and capable of taking a proactive military action against any enemy state that threatens to obstruct the trade routes. *Military action must be taken irrespective of all threats to set an example for any other state. By firmly taking action against trade obstructions, citizens develop more trust on LokPal.*

34   Keeping Chiefs of Armed Forces Happy

Narada continues "whether your armed forces' chief is filled with happiness and enthusiasm, valiant, intelligent, patient, pure-hearted, well cultured, loyal to their hierarchy and expert in their work." *These are the important qualities required in chief of the armed forces. LokPal needs to understand that and appoint his military chiefs in accordance with those qualities. All recruitments of armed forces must be carried out after due testing of each soldier. The chiefs must have shown exemplary service for most of his soldier career. Unless a soldier has not gone through the ranks of the military, he doesn't become qualified to lead the forces. LokPal must also be from a military background. Diplomacy is a military function, not a civilian function. Military guides diplomacy, not vice-a-versa. Diplomacy cannot function without the backing of military strength. LokPal is not only the topmost military person but is also the chief diplomatic officer.*

Narada understands that large armies need to have an organization and he is stressing empowerment at local leadership levels. Narada inquires "Whether the leaders of your armed forces are expert in all types of warfare, intelligent, clever, fearless, without any covetousness and full of valor. I hope you respect them according to their position and responsibility." *LokPal must ensure that a very strong training schedule is instituted for all military soldiers as well as their commanders. Every soldier and commander must have experience with every single weapon system of the state. Therefore, the armed forces must maintain minimum variety in their arsenal. The wars are won when the soldiers & commanders employ superior tactics & strategies on the battlefield. The generals & soldiers must be trained in all possible military strategies and also uniform tactics. Covert military tactics & strategies must be reserved for special forces directly under the command of the secret service of LokPal.*

Leadership has to be established at all levels, however, the qualities of a leader remain the same (responsibilities may vary). *The military organization structure must be flat with respect to the LokPal. All different military commanders must report directly to the LokPal. LokPal must regularly reshuffle deployment of armed forces across all borders and should regularly send them on military expeditions to win more wealth or to protect Sanatana Dharma in far off lands. Every military formation must be complete in all respects. Pandavas maintained five different armed forces under each of the brothers. Bhagavan Ram maintained four different armed forces to defeat Ravana.*

An army serves well when it is properly taken care of with proper weapons, and all other allied facilities needed for a quality life. *Soldiers must be regularly provided with new more advanced weapons in accordance with emerging strengths of enemies. Ideally, the LokPal must regularly diminish the military strength of the enemies through covert actions to ensure that his military is always superior to its enemies. An enemy in fear behaves like a friend. Military should be provided with all avenues of entertainment to ensure that they don't become looters in case of victory or defeat in war.*

Chiefs are happy when given proper respect and remuneration. The promotion criteria of chiefs must be transparent. Loyalty to the State and capability to win wars should be the only criteria for promotion. *All soldiers and their commanders should be provided with adequate remuneration in commensurate with their position. However, every commander must be given equal remuneration at any deployment. There should not be any gradation in remuneration. Therefore, armies must always be rotated as well as always deployed as per expedition. Military should never be peacetime deployed because that destroys their fighting skills.*

Soldiers must be selected based on their natural body characteristics based on the region from where they come from. Soldiers that can run fast must be deployed in plains and must be selected from similar lands. Soldiers recruited from mountainous regions must. be deployed in mountains. Navy must be selected from regions near the oceans or rivers where they are naturally good swimmers and also don't have fear of water. *All soldiers must be given the same training for loyalty to LokPal, loyalty to state, loyalty to Dharma and above all loyalty to Vedic teachers before they are given additional military skills. Every soldier must be trained to be a commander to ensure that the military of the state fights till the last soldier.*

35   Train your Armed forces Leaders

Narada continues,"Whether your different Generals of armed forces are expert in all types of warfare, clever, fearless, non covetous, and brave ? Do you honor and respect them as required?" *Narada is again emphasizing on the training and morale of the Armed forces of LokPal. Armed forces of LokPal help in protecting the Varnashrama system of the state. When Varnashrama is protected then automatically, Sanatana Dharma is protected. Pandavas would always discuss military strategies & tactics in their personal discussions amongst themselves. Every military leader must be highly educated and always ready & willing to wage a war against the enemies.*

LokPal must set up Defence colleges for all types of modern warfare and spycraft. *All defense colleges & research institutions must be set up near the regional recruitment centers so that prospective recruits get a flavor of military research culture. Defense colleges must be spread across all parts of the state. Soldiers must be trained to fight from the age of five years.* State must be prepared for war at all times to maintain peace. Soldiers must be evaluated for seven qualities before they are selected for military commission as mentioned in Bhagavad Gita - *'शौर्यं तेजो धृतिर्दाक्ष्यं युद्धे चाप्यपलायनम् । दानमीश्वरभावश्च क्षात्रं कर्म स्वभावजम् ॥ ४३ ॥ - Heroism, Power, Determination, Expertise, Never running from Battlefield, Daan (giving based on Guna), and Controlling & Managing qualities are the qualities & actions through which a Kshattriya is recognized.'*

Personal qualities that should be checked in Generals are

1. Loyalty to LokPal
2. Education of Dharma
3. Royal or Military family background

Technically educated soldiers add tremendous value in modern warfare and must be hired by the LokPal. *Yantra education must be compulsory for all soldiers & their commanders. All advanced weapons and their ammunition must be locally produced to enable the military to fight long term wars. Foreign made weapon systems reduce chances of victory in wars. All foreign weapon systems must be used only for short & small battles only. LokPal must always take the war to enemy territory to reduce risk to the citizens of his state.*

Generals must be totally dedicated to the state without any profit motive from the state. The LokPal must fire Generals freely if they present any doubtful dealing or character. After removal from position the general must not be allowed to leave the country. *No general whether retired or serving must ever connect with private profit making organizations because their services may be needed in case of war. They must be paid so well that there should never arise a situation that would seek any future civilian engagement. They should also not be allowed to leave the state except on military*

expeditions even after their retirement. All soldiers must be taught the history from Ramayana and Mahabharat so that they are willing to defend dharma at all times. In case a Military General becomes greedy for more money then that general must be imprisoned because he will foster corruption and may also join hands with the enemy. *The family members of the military personnel must be given attractive positions of responsibility within the state. Their members must be given preferential military positions if they are qualified.*

36   Morale of Armed Forces

Narada inquires"Whether you provide salaries in a timely manner to your armies and also the supply of quality food is maintained at all levels. I hope there is no delay and scarcity of supplies to your armed forces."

Morale of Defense forces need to be maintained high at all times, whether peace or at war. Salaries, Food, Logistics and Quality of Weapons play an important role in maintaining morale of armed forces. Excessive Delay in food and salaries is not taken lightly by employees. *Salaries to all soldiers must be paid on time at all times. That should be the top priority for the LokPal. In addition, quality food must be provided free to all serving & retired soldiers. Healthcare of all active & retired soldiers and their families should be free for lifetime if their families also serve the armed forces. The retired soldiers must be made responsible to main dharma in civilian areas at all times. They should also be employed as secret service to become the eyes & ears of LokPal.*

Morale of the armed forces is maintained by

1. Good Weapons
2. Good Food
3. Timely salaries
4. Good retirement benefits
5. Feelings of Loyalty to nation
6. Good training
7. Best intelligence
8. Protection of family at home when troops are deployed
9. Economic prosperity of nation
10. Trust in Political leadership especially LokPal

Lokpal must maintain his conduct so that he commands respect and loyalty from his troops at all levels. *LokPal's personal character and beliefs become an important source of motivation for soldiers. The more the LokPal is loyal to Dharma, the more the soldiers are loyal to him. This is the biggest secret of maintaining a strong military.*

Essential mantras for building a strong nation.

1. Military defends Dharma.
2. Dharma creates a State.
3. LokPal protects Dharma.
4. Dharma brings prosperity to the state.

The boundaries of the state are the boundaries of Dharma. The extent to which Dharma is practiced is the boundary of the state. Therefore, LokPal must always be focused on extending the boundaries where dharma can be peacefully practiced by all within the boundaries of that state. *The constant struggle between Dharma and Adharma motivates and sustains the motivation & morale of Armed forces of LokPal.*

37   Ensuring timely Salaries

Narada gives advice to LokPal Yudhishthir "Subjects become annoyed against their masters when there is excessive delay in salary and food. That anger may become the cause of great misfortune."

This is a very general observation for the collective good of the king and kingdom. A LokPal needs to ensure that his subjects basic needs are always met, otherwise his objectives will always remain unfulfilled. *LokPal must also ensure that the salaries of all civilian staff must always be paid on time. At Least one meal during the day must be provided by the LokPal to all his staff. Also on important occasions valuable gifts must be given to all state employees. Healthcare & Education must be free for all state employees and their families so that corruption can be eliminated in governance.*

Not just the armed forces, even other subjects must be given salary and food on time. The LokPal needs to ensure that all taxes are collected on time so that state employees are paid on time. LokPal needs to ensure that all state employees and citizens receive

- Free Healthcare

- Free Education
- Free food

Failure to take care of immediate subjects may result in dissatisfaction which may turn into open revolt against the LokPal. *LokPal must regularly communicate with his subjects through personal communications during public appearances. For subjects who have served for generations LokPal must make it a point to regularly personally interact with loyal subjects. Failure to do so will result in sowing the seeds of distrust amongst the subjects. Subjects must also be aware of severe punishment for disloyalty against dharma & state.*

38   Test for Loyalty

Narada further inquired " whether all ministers are born in good families and all other officials in your administration love you. I hope they are ready to lay down their lives for your sake." Successful administration works on loyalty and competence of close associates. *LokPal must always test his ministers & important officials for their loyalty to dharma & state. LokPal must also test their personal loyalty towards him. They should always be given tasks which test their love for LokPal.*

Narada wants to ensure whether King Yudhishthir understands this principle. Discipline makes a system work. *Discipline must be instituted in the system through a strict system of rewards & punishment. The system of rewards & punishment must be regularly practiced by the LokPal. Ministers act independently when they are assured of inaction by the LokPal. Then, those ministers act against the interest of the citizens, state, dharma and even LokPal. Therefore, LokPal must always demonstrate his willingness to act against errant ministers & officials to ensure fear of repercussions in their minds.*

Loyalty is always earned, cannot be commanded or bribed. The LokPal needs to maintain high moral and spiritual standards in public and private life to gain trust of citizens. Nepotism of any kind must be strictly avoided by the LokPal at all times.

LokPal gains the trust of his ministers through his personal exemplary example. When the LokPal becomes lazy in executing his own responsibilities, then it encourages sycophant ministers to become truant. LokPal must himself display his own loyalty to Dharma at all times. It is the following of Dharma that sustains LokPal's reputation. Dharma encompasses everything for a Lokpal. Dharma guides his military strategy, governance approach, culture, personal life and everything else that is needed to deliver outcomes to his citizens.

39   Firing Whimsical Military Officers

Narada next inquires from King Yudhisthira "whether any of your employees who work whimsically as per their own volition and regularly flout your decisions or decisions of your ministers. Whether your generals run your war operations alone or without following orders from their superiors." Emphasis is given by Narada on teamwork and discipline. It's important for a political leader to keep control of his subjects through discipline. At the same time, a political leader needs to reward their political subjects adequately. *LokPal must never tolerate indiscipline and insubordination at any time. Every instance of such action must carry a corresponding punishment for the truant employees.*

Indiscipline in armed forces must not be tolerated at any time. *Every single act of discipline must be punished with a commensurate military punishment. Military laws must be different from civilian laws. Military indiscipline is the most serious offense because it directly deals with the security of the state & LokPal. When military generals become truant then they must be immediately punished with capital punishment.*

Officers who work whimsically must be removed without any delay and strict court martial proceedings must be initiated immediately failing which there are dangers of coup. *The chances of military coup are very real for the LokPal. Therefore, the secret service of LokPal must always monitor the behavior of all military generals. Any type of loose comments or behavior must be treated as a forewarning. It is important for the LokPal to act before any small truancy could get out of hand. Therefore, LokPal must always be fully informed about all of his military leaders. Whimsical Military officers must be removed from all their responsibilities if the chances of correcting their behavior is not possible through any means.*

40   Award Individual Initiatives

Narada inquires," Do you reward your subjects who take initiatives on their own to deliver good work for you? Do you give him more recognition, higher pay and higher benefits?

It's important to reward high performers with more benefits and salaries. Educated and wise citizens must always be respected by the state. *LokPal must identify all those employees, officials and ministers who outperform in their outcomes. Failure to do so will encourage indifference amongst the subjects. Yudhishthir would always reward his officials with his personal jewelry.*

Anyone who takes individual initiative must be rewarded with

- A House
- A state pension, and
- A State vehicle for the duration of his or her life

All state subjects must be given a specific outcome to achieve. Attaining that outcome is a criterion for performing the job. However, when a subject attains at least 10% more than the target, then that subject becomes qualified to be rewarded. The outcomes are different for different subjects:

- Ministers must be given an outcome to either increase the boundaries of the state or increasing the treasury of the state
- Officials must be given an outcome to help attain the minister his outcome
- Military officials must be given an outcome of winning a battle

LokPal must also create a program to reward great saints of the country through recognition. *For that, LokPal must spend at least a day with them to listen to them and hear their concerns.*

41   Wise Citizens must be rewarded

Narada asks, "Do you reward your educated and wise citizens with wealth according to their knowledge, good qualities and wisdom? Because that's the way to give them recognition and respect."

Wise and educated citizens must be rewarded with

- State title
- State pension
- State House, and
- a State vehicle

State recognition is necessary to encourage other citizens to follow their lead. States must also provide free specialized education to the children of such citizens. A LokPal who doesn't reward his wise and educated citizens risks losing popularity in the eyes of citizens. *Wise citizens must be heard directly by the LokPal. LokPal must set up a time every month to invite them to the capital and listen to them individually or in a group. Special awards must be constituted to honor excellence in civilian life.*

LokPal must also watch for enemies influencing his wise citizens. These rewards are the way in which a LokPal stops the enemies' plan to create a revolt against him. *Citizens usually express themselves openly against the state when they are not heard by their government. All officials of the LokPal must be ordered to set up public meetings where they engage directly with educated citizens of the state. Then he must communicate those messages in their original form back to the LokPal.*

42   Military Families must be protected

Turning back to the welfare of Military personnel, Narada inquires," Do you properly take care of children of military personnel who give their lives willingly to your causes?". *Military is the most important arm of the state. The state that ignores military preparedness ceases to exist in due course of time.*

The welfare of military personnel is of paramount importance to the Political leadership. Any state that neglects the welfare of the family of military personnel often ceases to exist. *Ordinary civilians must be trained to respect the families of serving military personnel. Special days must be set up where the families of serving military personnel are respected in public.*

Especially families of those veterans who lay down their lives in the service of the state. Their children must be taken care of by the state. *Nowadays, Political Leadership fails to recognize the sacrifice of families of veterans, but in ancient times of Mahabharata, the LokPal was directly responsible for the welfare of families of veterans. All immediate family members of fallen soldiers must be provided with state jobs and other state benefits for their supreme sacrifice in the service of dharma.*

The head of State needs to protect even those enemies who surrender out of either fear or destruction of personal property. *The eldest child of the defeated enemy was enthroned in place of their father. In that way, enmity is removed from the root. The war must always be proactively fought to protect dharma, even in the enemy state. The LokPal must not turn a blind eye to adharma in any part of the world. LokPal must be ready to use his military forces anywhere in the world to protect dharma. That becomes a main reason for 'moksha (liberation from karma cycle)' for LokPal.*

Not only the LokPal needs to protect the families of those who risk their lives for the state but also of the enemies who surrender. *Even the families of those enemies who have surrendered must be provided full state protection by the LokPal. When the families of surrendered enemies are protected then they become grateful to LokPal and further help in revealing more information about the enemy.* LokPal must always be kind to everyone who has taken shelter of him.

43   Fallen Enemies must be sheltered

Narada inquires," Do you protect those enemies who take your shelter out of fear of losing? Do you protect those enemies who fear vandalism or destruction of their personal property? Especially those enemies who have been defeated by you in war? Do you protect those enemies as you would protect your own children?"

This instruction shows the magnanimity in which a head of state should function. This is even better than any Vienna conventions that the modern world follows. In the age of Mahabharata, the protection of a defeated enemy was directly entrusted to the head of state. *Fallen enemies must be sheltered within the territory of the enemy. After winning a war, the LokPal must always carve out a small area in the enemy territory for settling the fallen enemies and also surrendered enemies. Retired military personnel must also be settled in those areas to ensure dharma is maintained.*

This instruction should provide guidance to the United Nations to improve the quality of protection for state forces. However, it will be a challenge to establish such rules for terrorists because of their ideological hatred based military missions. For such terrorists, a criminal punishment is required outside the purview of state sponsored care. The current international law works against Dharma.

Yudhishthira was the de facto ruler of Earth during the times of Mahabharata[35]. Personal popularity of the head of the State is established by his ability to derive confidence from the masses. *The confidence on the LokPal arises when LokPal shows kindness to all.*

When families of enemies are protected, it helps the LokPal to expand his intelligence network in the enemy state. LokPal must be ever ready to protect enemies for the sake of protecting his own state. The LokPal needs to know whether a foreign ideology of any type is meant to weaken his administration or weaken social harmony within his state. *Kindness is the dharma of LokPal. Only a very strong LokPal can show kindness.*

Such ideologies must be rejected and thrown out of his state. Incompatibility of ideologies creates disturbance in the state and it becomes a cause of great distress to its citizens. *All those who oppose dharma are naturally the enemies of LokPal. LokPal must wage military campaigns even against those who are ideologically against Dharma. Fear of military action brings those enemies under control.*

44 Ensuring Universal Trust

Narada inquires,"O leader of Earth, do all the inhabitants of earth regard you equanimously and trust you as good as their own parents? The comparison to parental trust is significant here. Because a child has a maximum trust in parents.

That trust is the barometer for comparing other trusts. The head of State has to build that trust with every citizen of the country. Yudhisthira was able to build that kind of trust with all citizens of the entire Earth because of his personal qualities, his knowledge and his military prowess. *The personal qualities of the LokPal build trust of the masses on him.*

At the same time, the head of state is responsible to provide security to his state subjects. One of the essential aspects of providing security to his state subjects is through controlling the state enemies. *When a LokPal provides security to all, then the LokPal becomes a King in the eyes of the subjects. When security is strong then it empowers the common citizens to practice dharma in their own lives.*

Every official of the state must be protected by

- State secret service
- State army where necessary

Special zones must be created to protect all important citizens. All citizens must also be trained to protect themselves with personal weapons. State must keep a track on all personal weapons owned and operated by citizens.

Weapons must be allowed in the hands of trained and mentally sound people. When good citizens are armed and protected then thieves & other anti-social elements are not allowed to fester in the society. The concept of policing is not needed when citizens & judiciary are authorized to prevent criminality in the society. Even terrorism based on artificial religious superiority can be defeated through armed and aware citizenry.

45   Observing Enemies' personal Faults

Narada inquires from Yudhishthir, "Do you constantly keep a watch whether your enemy is engaged in bad habits such as gambling or too much attached to women? If they are engaged in such weaknesses do you constantly try to examine their strengths and weaknesses? Do you keep a watch on your enemies' three strengths viz Strength of Resources, Strength of Enthusiasm and Strength of Good Counsel? If after due consideration, you find that the enemy is weak, do you attack them with your full strength? " *It's important for the Head of State to know the art of Warfare. The art of warfare is the content of this book also. The best sources of such information comes from Mahabharata & Ramayana. By constantly observing the movement of enemies and taking small military covert actions against those officials, a larger war is averted.*

Attacking the enemy when it is weak is the most opportune moment to gain victory. The personal character of the head of State is extremely important in determining the strength of the state itself. *Attacking and completely destroying the military capability of the enemy when they are weak is a wise strategy for the LokPal.*

There are three main strengths of the Head of State, and analyzing them is the key to understanding the strength of a state. *The strength of the state comes from the LokPal, who follows dharma.*

- Resource Strength: A state is known by its large repository of wealth, armed forces and its friendly states. A collection of all three determines if a state is powerful or not. A state rich in all three is considered stable.

  A state needs to maintain a strong military and internal law enforcement. In addition to that it needs to maintain strong allies who can help when needed.

- Counsel Strength: A head of state is as powerful as its advisors. If advisors or council of advisors is strong then the Head of State is well protected from State's enemies.

  Therefore it's advisable that a head of state keeps good advisors on its payrolls. A good advisor multiplies the strength of the Head of State. A good counsel is worth many times over a general counsel.

- Enthusiasm Strength: The enthusiasm of the subjects of the Head of State is important for the enthusiasm of the State.

Lack of enthusiasm in a state happens due to three reasons:

- ➤ Corruption: Corruption is the biggest enemy of any state. It makes the state empty from within.
  - ○ Three places where corruption resides in a state are Bureaucracy, Health Systems and Judiciary. If these three institutions are properly controlled then the state becomes a success.
- ➤ Weak Armed Forces

- ○ State needs to maintain a strong internal law enforcement and also a strong army ready for invading other lands
- ○ Weak Institutions: Public Welfare, Education, Health, Judiciary are the pillars of social stability.

LokPal must carefully study all sources of strength as well as enthusiasm of the enemy. LokPal must do everything possible to reduce the military fighting capability of the enemy when they are building their capacity. LokPal must evaluate whether the enemy is following dharma or is engaged in adharma. LokPal must make friends with them if they are following dharma. If the enemy is engaged in adharma, then the LokPal must send spies to infiltrate all their sources of enthusiasm as well as strengths. LokPal must weaken them completely from within to ensure that their military strength is one-third of his. Then the LokPal must wage a direct military action to militarily defeat them and merge their territory with his. *Failure to do so at the right time will result in the downfall of LokPal.*

46   Twelve Officials of Enemy

Narada inquires further,"O destroyer of enemies, do you recognize the twelve key groups of officials in your enemies? Do you know what activities you need to perform? Do you analyze your own weaknesses and your enemies weaknesses? If you find that your enemy is weak at an opportune time, I hope you attack them while depending on deva[36] and paying advance salaries to soldiers." *When the military is engaged in operations then their salaries must be doubled as a special benefit. LokPal must always be faithful to Devatas as well as great vedic saintly people in his state. Before engaging in war, he should take care of all steps necessary to weaken the enemy. Then, LokPal should always pray to Durga for her blessings in war. Then, LokPal must consult his Guru before launching the military expedition.*

The twelve groups are mentioned as

1. Two enemies of enemy (2)
2. Two friends of enemy (2)
3. Two friends above two categories (2)
4. Two Soldiers guarding the frontier (2)
5. One sad advisor of enemy (1)
6. One depressed advisor of enemy (1)
7. Two chief motivators of enemy (2)

The head of state has to continuously monitor these 12 groups of people on both his side and his enemies' side. *These twelve groups of enemy officials must be constantly observed and followed at all times. In the case of military operation, all of these twelve groups must be simultaneously attacked.*

It is the duty of the Head of State to observe following people from his enemy states:

1. One who is greedy. And also those who haven't been paid proper salaries
2. One who is respected but has been insulted
3. One who is prone to become angry and has been insulted beyond control to become mad with anger
4. One who is fearful, and have been scared more by the enemies

LokPal must buy the loyalty of all those who can be bought in the enemy state. There should be no leniency shown to enemies. When the LokPal shows leniency to enemies then that increases their enthusiasm.

Danger to the state comes from two broad categories:

A. Daiva[37] (दैव)
   a. Fire
   b. Water
   c. Disease
   d. Sudden Calamities
   e. Widespread Epidemic
B. Manush[38] (मानुष)
   a. Foolish persons
   b. Thieves
   c. Enemies of State
   d. Beloved Close associates of the King
   e. Fear due to a greedy king

To protect from Daiva, LokPal must regularly conduct Yagya in his state for those devatas. By conducting Yagyas, Lokpal increases his piety which helps in increasing the mental and spiritual strength of LokPal. When a LokPal performs yagya in his state then the natural calamities reduce. LokPal must also ensure that there is no mass killing of animals, birds & aquatics in the state for food. To protect the state from other humans, LokPal must create a very strong judiciary based on Dharma to give proper punishments to all miscreants. LokPal must be confident in executing his responsibilities towards dharma because that ensures his success in creating prosperity for all in the state.

47   Honoring Top Military Commanders

Narada then continues, "I hope you regularly give valuable gifts to your top commanders of armed forces according to their levels in your armed forces." *Narada is instructing Yudhishthir on properly honoring the military commanders in his forces. All military commanders must have direct individual direct interaction with the LokPal. That enables the LokPal to understand the enthusiasm of his military. That's why a flat military structure at the top helps LokPal lead decisive victory in battles.*

Narada emphasizes to retain the loyalty of top commanders to maintain morale in his armed forces. Also, the gifts have to be commensurate with the position of the commander. *The loyalty of top commanders comes when all commanders trust the loyalty of LokPal to dharma. Top commanders must also be convinced of the military credentials of the LokPal. They must know that LokPal himself is capable of winning any war. That respect makes military commanders loyal to the LokPal. In addition, when the LokPal respects their loyalty and military leadership through gifts and awards, then the military commanders would even want to give their life to protect dharma for LokPal.* Flag of a nation represents the dharma of a nation. The symbols on the flag must represent the native culture of the land. *The symbols of native culture on the flag elicit the loyalty of military commanders towards dharma.*

When the flag is disrespected then the dharma of the land is disrespected. Every military commander must be allowed to choose his own flag for the force he commands to personally motivate him to serve dharma. *When LokPal allows such freedoms to his military commanders then he gains further trust of the commander. LokPal must never be insecure about the loyalty of his commanders and must be willing to himself take over the command whenever he wishes to do it. Every land also has a dharma and therefore the symbols of the original local native culture must be represented in the flag. In Mahabharata & Ramayana, every military commander had their unique flag to motivate their forces. But they all collectively fought for dharma.* When the LokPal enters a battle then he must also carry his flag to motivate all the troops of all commanders.

48 Engaging Enemy Military officers

Narada continues,"Whether you identify key warriors in your enemy state and secretly give them jewels and other financial benefits to win them over to your side?".

LokPal must keep a list of all principal warriors of the enemy and keep updating that list as and when changes happen. There must be At Least three spies keeping a watch on every key warrior of the enemy. *The enemy military officers must be profitably engaged by the secret services of LokPal. They must be given wealth to enjoy vacation in different places outside of the state of LokPal. Their family members must be given access to excessive sense enjoyment so much so that they relish a life of luxury.*

If possible, each warrior of enemy must be

- Honey trapped to provide intelligence
- Given money and jewels for their wives and children
- Provided free education

When the enemy is controlled, prosperity reigns for LokPal and his state. *LokPal engages enemy military officers so that they refuse to fight when the need arises. The enemy military officers must speak about peace so that the morale of their forces are always weak.*

In the eventuality of actual war, LokPal must protect such military officers of the enemies by giving them shelter in a special land carved out of their own country. *The military of LokPal must destroy all other enemy military officers in a war who refused to cooperate with him.*

49   Personal Sense Control

Narada continues,"Whether you win over your mind and senses before you desire to win over your bewildered and intoxicated enemies?".

Personal character of the King is of paramount importance in governing a land. Every Head of State must try to control their mind through Yoga and other yogic meditation processes. *The LokPal must be a yogi. Without Yog, LokPal won't be able to efficiently & expertly execute his responsibilities. Yog entails complete control over mind & intelligence. Yog makes LokPal a superior person amongst the comity of all leaders within his state. Unless the LokPal conquers his own mind, senses & intelligence, he won't be able to conquer enemies of the state whether internal or external.*

Also, sense control is of utmost importance for the success of the head of state. The real complete victory is obtained through a personal sense of control. *LokPal is allowed to engage in controlled sense enjoyment. But when the LokPal controls his senses through Yog, then automatically he is beloved by masses as well as his ministers & officials.*

Usually, heads of state are advised by Narada Muni to

1. Control senses
2. Control mind
3. Control intelligence

A personal regimen of meditation is a must for every single LokPal. Morning time must be utilized in meditation on Harinam and reading of Bhagavad Gita. *Bhagavad Gita is the most important source of information on Yog to LokPal. It summarizes the entire science of Yog in a few words. Every LokPal must spend his time reading Gita and trying to understand it from authorized sources. Most of the free time of LokPal must be spent in hearing or reading Mahabharata & Ramayana.*

50   Seven Solutions

Narada then inquires,"Whether you consider Diplomacy, Charity/Gifts, Differentiation and Punishment in that order, before you attack your enemies. Because to control your enemies, these strategies are important to use."

These strategies are only used to protect Dharma or righteousness based on vedic scriptures. These strategies are vital to control enemies of Dharma.

Diplomacy: It is the first step in resolving political disputes. Diplomacy involves transactional exchanges for a win-win solution to all parties involved. It can succeed only if both parties reasonably work to address the core issues through negotiations. One of the important characteristics of Diplomacy is civilized conversations stating respective positions. Sophisticated total communication is the necessity of Diplomacy. *This solution works only when LokPal has a strong offensive military posture against his enemies. Fear of military repercussions makes diplomacy work. LokPal must never keep his enemies in peace by assuring them of peace before diplomacy. Diplomacy is the art of keeping peace. LokPal's military must be at the doorsteps of the enemy before the dialogue is started.*

Charity/Gifts: When Diplomacy fails, then the second strategy of transactional relationship building begins when both parties exchange items of value to come to an agreement. This is the most useful strategy in today's times. *LokPal must use this solution to completely buy out officials of the enemy. Keeping them on his payroll, LokPal may bring sense to them to avoid military confrontation.*

Differentiation: When none of the above strategies work, then it's advisable to create confusion in the ranks of enemies. *Creating confusion amongst the ranks of enemies helps in disorienting. This is done through various information channels in the enemy state. LokPal must infiltrate the enemy completely at all times to be able to use this strategy.*

Punishment: This is a last resort, when everything else as mentioned above fails. This is where the Head of State is advised to wage a war to achieve its dharmic state objectives. *This solution needs to be employed against all those who flout the dharma. Generally, this involves using the judiciary to adjudicate internal miscreants. This involves using the full military might of the state against external enemies.*

Mantra: Mantras are great solutions because they involve blessings from higher beings such as Devatas and their assistants. *Society doesn't prosper without Yagyas. Yagyas are done to please devatas. LokPal must make facilities for citizens where they congregate to chant vedic mantras. Such actions increase the popularity of LokPal.*

Aushadhi: Aushadhi means vegetables, flowers, fruits, green leafy vegetables, spices and others are considered aushadhi. *Ayurveda mentions them as a solution for building a healthy society. Aushadhi serves as medicine as well as poison. LokPal must also develop counter-poison medicines for everyone in his state. LokPal must also build poisons to be used against enemies.*

Indrajaal: Indrajaal means strategy that cannot be overcome by any enemy. *The game of chatur-rang which was later known as shatranj by Zoroastrians was the original game of strategy taught to all those involved in managing the state. This game was revived by Chanakya when he created the modern day Chess which he taught to his illustrious student, Chandragupta Maurya. Indrajaal needs to be employed against all internal as well as external enemies of the state & dharma.*

These seven solutions have to be utilized to increase the power of the state. LokPal must ensure that the enemy is fully aware of the enormous military defeat if that enemy chooses to work against the state of LokPal. This is the dharma of LokPal.

51   Securing Home

Narada next inquires, "Whether you make your country foundationally secure before you attack your enemies? I hope you put all your resources to use to subdue your enemy. And after winning victory over your enemies, you provide them with security."

It is important for the head of state to be brave to take courageous decisions. Nation states are built on the strong leadership of the leader. *LokPal must always make the enemy nervous through a dissuasive & offensive military capability. LokPal must never hesitate to not use the military to extract submission from the enemy. LokPal must also make his intention of acquiring enemies' lands in the case of military operation.*

The five pillars of a state are

1. Dharma
2. Military
3. Finance
4. Administration
5. Education

These five pillars rest on the foundation of security. With a good foundation and good pillars, citizens live happily and then they can focus on spiritual advancement. The whole purpose of a stable nation state is to provide facilities to the citizens for spiritual growth. *The external & internal security of the state lies in the hands of internal & external security apparatus. LokPal must clearly define who the external & internal enemies of the state are.*

LokPal must regularly update this information based on the inputs of his secret service.

LokPal needs to use all his power to subdue his enemy and then provide shelter to those enemies who surrender. *The enemy soldiers must know that they will be secure when they surrender. LokPal must physically demonstrate this to show his intentions clearly. Before the beginning of the war, a special zone for prisoners of war must be set up with modern facilities. All captured soldiers must be kept there with no facilities of any outside communication.* When LokPal follows these seven solutions, then he always remains popular with the enemies as well his own subjects.

52 Maintaining Powerful Army

Narada next inquires, "Whether your armies well equipped with Treasurer, Chemists, Doctors, Spies, Cooks, Service Volunteers, Writers & Guards, Foot Soldiers, Cavalry, Elephants & Chariots, managed by well qualified Military Generals, are able to destroy the enemies of your state."

Narada Muni wants to ensure that the armies of Yudhishthir are well balanced and therefore suited to win any war. *LokPal must not only build a very offensive military organization but also focus on building a balanced force which can be offensive as well as able to retain territory. It is always a soldier that fights a war. Machines & Technology are just the tools that are given to a soldier to assist him in warfare.* The six administrative parts of a balanced military are

1. Strong Finances
2. Good Chemists and Pharmacists
3. Doctors
4. Good Secret Services
5. Excellent Cooks
6. Writers & Guards

The six features of a balanced military are

1. Infantry
2. Air and Space capabilities
3. Navy
4. Land Forces
5. Intelligence
6. Logistics

The organization of these divisions and strengths needs to be left to professionals in those respective fields. The pillar of a stable state is in its military prowess. *Logistics plays an important role in maintaining high morale of the armed forces. The military must employ the best cooks to feed the soldiers even in remotest deployments. The logistics must precede any deployment. Also, the LokPal must plan military operations only after the entire logistics for winning the war in the worst scenario is ready. The logistics must also include war historians as well as volunteers for medical help when needed.* LokPal must use all dissuasive postures before strategically attacking the most vulnerable part of the enemy. The enemy must not know where the attack would happen first. *By building a balanced military, LokPal ensures military victory in all wars.*

53   Enemies must be destroyed

Narada continues, "Whether you kill your enemies in battle without considering their harvest time and drought if case be."

This is an important reminder to remove any mental weakness of the leader. Leader is supposed to show valor in battle. Any considerations of emotional weakness due to the drought or famine while the war is going on can result in defeat. A leader needs to plan everything before going to war to ensure victory is achieved. *Enemy must never be left alive. Leaving an enemy alive becomes the reason for a much worse war in future. Every war that LokPal initiates must be decisive and conclusive, otherwise, the war must never be initiated.*

Until the enemy state is completely destroyed, a LokPal should not rest. Not just enemy states but also individuals who pose as enemies. *LokPal must never be kind to an enemy that has refused all avenues of peace. Enemy must also know that outcome. While destroying the enemies, LokPal must leave aside all emotional weakness or any care for the enemy once the military operations have begun. All chances of peace are before the war begins, after that, the only option that the LokPal has is to win the war. LokPal must never accept any peace deal during the war. Once the LokPal has satisfactorily won the war, should the LokPal discuss any peace treaty after retaining all the lands that he has won during the war. Failure to do so will result in infamy of the LokPal in the history books.*

The leader has to be emotionally and spiritually strong to make good decisions. The good decisions come when a leader takes care of two guiding principles:

1. Benefit for Masses: A leader must protect the interests of all people in his constituency
2. Dharma or Law of the Land: A leader must uphold the sanctity of the rule of law as commonly accepted

No mercy is ever given to enemies of the State or LokPal. Mercy given to enemies of state emboldens the enemy more.

54   Spycraft

Narada then inquires, "Whether your state officials roam from place to place in your state and your enemy states to maintain discipline in the society, perform other state duties and also collect taxes. Do your officials also protect people favorable to you and also those who increase the security of your state?"

It is the duty of all leaders to create a lean team for performing multiple duties for the welfare of the citizens. Large governments are usually not advised by Narada muni because it moves people away from the government. Also it creates more tax burden on the citizens. *LokPal must ask all his officials and ministers to constantly tour across the entire length & breadth of the state. The chief task of the state officials should be to offer solutions to the local problems. Also, officials must also include other tasks such as inspection of local granaries and local water supply. The same officials must be also tasked with collecting taxes. No separate taxation team must be set up because that instills fear in the masses.*

So even in those times, an official of the state used to perform multiple tasks. Also, it builds the credibility of the leader. The official is an important communication medium for the leader. An in-person communication is far more effective than a non-personal communication. *All official communication should be in person followed by a state gazette. State officials must always protect law-abiding citizens favorable to dharma and LokPal. This increases support for the LokPal in the masses.*

Here the three takeaways for the Leader are:

1. Multi-tasking for State Officials

2. In-person communication with masses
3. Officials must be present in enemy states as well

An efficient intelligence department ensures security for the state and LokPal. The LokPal must also send his officials secretly to the border regions of enemy states as well. By doing so, LokPal learns about the status of dharma in the enemy territory. *LokPal must not only run his own state as per dharma but also ensure that dharma is followed in all neighboring states as well. When adharma is prominent in neighboring states, then that is sure to enter the state of LokPal as well.* LokPal must not only ensure dharma in his own state as well as neighboring states and especially, enemy states.

55   Self-protection

Narada then inquires, "Whether your eatables, clothes and perfumes/colognes are protected by capable and trustworthy people?"

This inquiry assumes significance because many Heads of States who have done important work for their people have been assassinated by their enemies. *LokPal must never eat outside in public view. LokPal must always serve food to his guests in public. LokPal must only eat food prepared by those trustworthy cooks who have served him and his family for generations. All prepared foods must be fed to pets in the house in front of LokPal before those are presented in front of LokPal. The secret service of LokPal must check every food that is presented for the consumption of LokPal. Ideally, a LokPal must always eat food in solitude. Nobody should know the food that LokPal consumes, nor his likes & dislikes in food.*

The leaders have to ensure that they are protected so that they can serve the larger interests of their people. It is this fact pointed out by Narada Muni. The personal items of the leader need to be protected by close and trusted confidants of the leader. LokPal's clothes must be tailored by tailors who have served LokPal's family for generations. *LokPal must never accept foreign clothes which have been gifted to him. LokPal must only wear those clothes which are made as per local tastes and fashions. LokPal must always dress opulently to instill confidence in the masses.*

Ideally perfumes and any other lotion or ointment should never be imported for LokPal. *Perfumes & other ointments can be poisoned by enemies. Therefore, LokPal must exercise all precautions before using any cologne which has been imported. Ideally, the secret service of LokPal must always refuse such gifts from foreign nations.*

All personal use items must be made under a strict supervision of LokPal's confidante aids. *All personal use items such as shaving creams, soaps, shampoos, oils and others, must be procured from specialized non-commercial vendors. LokPal must never use any personal items which are sold for the general public.* Even the closest ministers & officials must not know the type or category of personal use items of the LokPal. LokPal and his secret service must observe topmost secrecy about the personal items used by the LokPal.

56   Protecting State Reserves

Narada then inquires, "Whether your treasury, granary, main doors, weapons and other tools of income are well protected and taken good care of by loyal, endeavoring, and competent people who are always working hard for your welfare?"

Here the qualification of the most trusted officers of the LokPal is mentioned. The leader needs to identify hard working officers who have his interest paramount in their minds. Loyalty and Competence go hand in hand for all workers of a state. *The state secret service must protect all granaries, doors, weapons and other avenues of income. The security of all these assets of LokPal must never be shown to the public ostensibly. Rather, retired military officials and responsible citizens must be the physically visible officials. Those who are given state pensions, must be employed to secure important assets in public view.*

The important points of interest are:

1.   Treasury
2.   Ports of Entry
3.   Granaries
4.   Weapons and Ammunition Depots
5.   Defense Installations
6.   Important Departments of State

These six sections of state are important to be entrusted to trustworthy people. *Those who have served the nation must be further trusted to secure these important assets of the state. The secret service must use all types of tools and technologies to ensure both internal and external security of institutions of the state. The state intelligence apparatus must also secure these installations from enemies of the state.* A LokPal who secures these six symbols of the state defeats all enemies.

57   Self-protection from internal Enemies

Narada then inquires, "Whether you protect yourself from your cooks, bodyguards, Internal Palace workers and armed chiefs, before anyone else? After you ensure your safety, do you ensure the safety of your loved ones and also from all of the above category of state workers?"

The Head of State not only needs to protect his important departments of state but also ensure the safety of himself and his close relatives. *LokPal must employ secret service to protect himself from all workers in his residence as well as office. However, there should be a separate personal security bodyguard force whose only task is to ensure the complete protection of LokPal.*

The leader needs to ensure that his safety is more important for the state than anything else. The head of State is also referred to as Caretaker of the State and its subjects. *The secret service of the LokPal must also protect immediate & distant family members from all types of enemies. The secret service of the LokPal must extend their security to the family of LokPal even from the workers of their own residence.*

Here important responsibilities of LokPal are:

1. Head of State is the caretaker of the state
2. Head of State is responsible for his own and his family's security also

LokPal must always take care of his citizens like a father. But at the same time ensure security for himself and his family from enemies that may infiltrate his citizenry.

58 Morning time is Special

Narada then inquires,"Whether you waste your time and money in Alcohol, Gambling, Sports, and Young women and other bad habits early in the morning?"

The personal habits of a king play an important role in managing the affairs of the state. It is advised that the head of state wakes up early before sunrise and must avoid the morning time for any sense gratification habits. *Entertainment is extremely important for a LokPal. However, morning time should be avoided for all such activities. Morning time is reserved for Yog and other vedic ritualistic ceremonies.*

Time and money are very important commodities to be saved by a king. Time is money and money buys time. Both have to be used wisely and effectively. Good money invites good money and bad money invites bad money. *All relationships with different women must be kept a personal secret by the LokPal. It is the duty of the secret service of the LokPal to shield him from all prying eyes. LokPal must construct separate residences where he entertains himself.*

Quality of People (QoP) determines the quality of money. Time saved is money earned. Money spent wisely is time earnt. This is true in all situations. Ancient wisdom, modern application leads to prosperity for all. When a LokPal maintains a balanced lifestyle then he becomes dear to his citizens as well as ministers & officials. But LokPal must never engage in frivolous entertainment in the morning. *If a LokPal doesn't maintain discipline in his life then that LokPal definitely fails in future.*

59   Managing Finances

Narada then inquired, "Whether you are able to manage all your expenditures of the state in one-fourth or one-half or three-fourths of your monthly income?"

It is important for the head of state to know how to manage the state and his subjects economically. Economic expertise is one of the main skill sets of the head of state since time immemorial. *LokPal must always receive the reports about the economic condition of his state every morning. After completing his daily morning Yog schedule, LokPal must carefully study all economic indicators telling him the status of his economy. At the same time, LokPal must also review the intelligence reports and also reports of his military preparation. After reviewing these reports, LokPal must eat his breakfast.*

Economics drives the stability of the Kingdom and Stability leads to the spiritual side of the state. Everything is interconnected. Strong economy also leads to a strong military capability of the state. Budgetary financial management of the state is recommended to achieve the state's long term objectives. *LokPal must always manage his entire state in just half, one-fourth or three-fourths of all gross tax receipts. Ideally, the LokPal should not use more than one-half of all tax receipts. But LokPal must use at least one-fourth of all tax receipts. Fifty percent of balance tax receipts must be used in keeping all enemies in check. Fifty percent of the balance left must be used for military modernization and war funds. The balance left must be added back to the treasury for further use in any eventuality.*

The chief accountant of the state must tell the LokPal about the situation of state finances, every morning to the LokPal. If LokPal doesn't receive that information in the morning, then that accountant must be replaced. *LokPal must only appoint those accountants who are only interested in increasing the treasury of the LokPal. Accountants must not have a free hand in spending the money. LokPal must replace any accountant who argues with him on spending on welfare of his citizens as well as the military. Accountants should never have any say in policy matters of the state.* LokPal must reward an accountant who helps in increasing the treasury of the state.

60   Taking care of loved ones financially

Narada then inquires,"Whether you are able to financially take care of the needs of your close relatives, elderly, teachers, businessmen, artisans, and also distressed people? Are you constantly bestowing them with financial benefits to keep them loyal to you?"

It is the duty of the Head of state to constantly bestow financial favors to all his close associates. This provides a safety buffer to help King manage the state subjects. This is a very important technique to maintain loyalty and commitment. *LokPal must never keep his family members and relatives wanting for money. If that happens, then those family members can easily be infiltrated by the enemy.*

All close relatives and workers of the state must receive financial rewards from LokPal. Failure to provide such rewards results in disloyalty. *LokPal must pay monthly stipends to all members of the family. LokPal must also ensure that the family members do not exploit the state resources for frivolous expenditures. Ideally, LokPal must employ them in productive functions of the state under other competent officials & ministers.*

61 Accurate Financial Reporting

Narada then inquires,"Whether your accountants and analysts who are responsible for daily administrative tasks provide you a financial summary report to you of the state of the economy every morning."

The head of state must receive the state of economy briefing every morning before anything else. The economy is the most important aspect of management of state affairs. All accountants must report their progress to the King every morning. *At Least three ministers from the cabinet must review the financial reports every morning before presenting them to LokPal. After the review, LokPal must carefully read the reports himself to take further actions. If the report is favorable then the LokPal must give congratulatory messages to everyone in his cabinet. If the reports are unfavorable then he should task those three ministers for corrective action.*

Lekhak[39] and Ganak[40] means a writer and an accountant. Both of them must keep the LokPal completely informed on all aspects of diplomacy and financial situations. *The writer or historian must carefully present the important news from the entire state to the LokPal. That report must have all bad news, all good news as well as the status of Dharma in the society. This report must be read aloud later during the first part of the day before noon in the entire assembly.* Failure to do so will result in loss of accountability in the state.

62   Vigilance and Investigation

Narada then inquires, "Whether you not remove your expert, hard working, well wisher and beloved workers from jobs before properly investigating their offenses?"

Vigilance and Investigation are two important departments of State power. Every nation must maintain very strong vigilance operations for all of their employees. *LokPal must investigate every single report against his competent, honest and loyal officials. If any instance of lack of credibility is found in those complaints then a disciplinary action must be taken against the source of such complaint.*

Any slackness of vigilance will lead to lack of confidence for the King and his administration. Investigation of vigilance reports is also an important function of the state. Usually a separate department is required to maintain impartiality of investigations. *A separate department under his secret service must be set up to ensure proper follow up against every single instance of a complaint. LokPal must personally review all instances of such reports.*

Finally, King is the ultimate bestower of justice based on the report submitted by these two departments. Corruption in the state increases when these two departments are weak. *LokPal*

must ensure that all his vigilance officials are above any doubt on their integrity and loyalty to him. All investigative officers must be well versed in dharma as well as carry a mathematical precision in their process of investigation.

63   Grading and Engaging People

Narada then inquired, "Whether you identify hires in three categories such as Uttam (Top), Medium (Madhyam), Low (Adham) and engage them in work according to their levels?"

Every state employee must be categorized into three levels based on their competence, experience and loyalty. Not everyone is at the same level. The state administration must regularly promote or demote employees as per those three parameters of performance evaluation. *Gradation of employees gives a growth path to the employees. The promotion of employees must be strictly based on merit and loyalty. Every grade must carry separate perks and salaries to further motivate employees. All employees must be engaged as per Varna (classification of professions) and Ashram (four social orders). By employing Varnashrama, unemployment is completely eradicated from the state.*

Good employees must be rewarded and bad ones demoted both financially and position wise. *LokPal must always demote as well as promote employees. The criterion for demotion and promotion must be publicly known. Generally, the ministers must be chosen from employees who have demonstrated expertise in their chosen fields over the years of honest public life.* For exemplary employees, LokPal must also keep an option to appoint them as Governors of their respective regions.

64   Avoiding Unqualified People

Narada then inquires, "Whether you haven't employed people who have less experience, greed, thieves, enemies and are practically unqualified for any work?"

Kings should always employ people with impeccably clean records. *Intelligence & Vigilance reports must be reviewed for every official before that official is appointed, promoted or even demoted. LokPal must never over rule the intelligence reports even when the official may be personally known to him. LokPal must never trust his gut instincts over the factual ground reports by his departments.*

The three areas where a King needs needs to maintain the quality are:

- Relevant Experience: Practical experience of the role is called relevant experience
- Relevant Competence: Educational and Ideological Qualification for the role
- Lack of Greediness: Resistance against temptation tests the greediness aptitude of a person. The higher the resistance, the less greedy a person will be. Every prospective employee needs to be tested on this attribute.

Anytime a state employee should be demoted or removed from office if found lacking in competence, loyalty and experience. *LokPal must never hesitate to punish errant officials in any situation. Failure to do so fosters corruption in his state.* Failure to remove unqualified employees results in

- Failure of state
- Decrease in popularity of LokPal

Any LokPal who regularly takes actions against unqualified officials gains respect in the eyes of the public that he serves.

65   Avoiding Hurting your own State

Narada then inquires,"Whether you have ensured that you yourself are not hurting your kingdom? I hope you ensure that thieves, greedy people, princes, women of the palace don't hurt your state? Are your farmers content?"

LokPal needs to watch out for himself more than others to protect the state. Weakening of state institutions weakens the state. King's loved ones and family are the next most immediate threat to the state. Farmers are the bread producers of a state. The direct question about their welfare proves that Narada gives utmost importance to agriculture, the only industry that feeds the state directly. *If a LokPal is not following dharma properly then he becomes an enemy to his own state. The council of ministers and also the Guru of LokPal must ask that truant LokPal to step down after choosing a qualified Dharmic LokPal. LokPal must therefore always be the biggest protector of dharma in the state.*

Sometimes, LokPal may find himself to be in the way of the prosperity of the state. *LokPal is the topmost economist of the state. When the economic policies of the LokPal do not yield good results, then LokPal must consult his ministers and officials for corrective action. LokPal must heed to their suggestions without being overly attached to his viewpoints. Failure to do so will result in LokPal becoming an obstruction on the path of prosperity to his own state.*

At that time, LokPal needs to recuse himself from the work of the state and go for

- Education
- Meditation, and or

- Hunting
- Association with Vedic teachers

Such small vacations help a LokPal in strengthening his mind & intellect to make better policies for his state.

LokPal must always be ready to renounce the state for a better LokPal. That quality of renunciation makes LokPal extremely dear to his citizens. *Ideally, LokPal must only be attached to Dharma. LokPal must not be attached to his reputation, his likes or dislikes and even to his own honor. LokPal must also not be attached to his past record because such attachments obstruct the vision of the future.*

LokPal must always act against thieves, society women of the palace and other greedy people from his palace. *Failure to do so results in loss of mandate for the LokPal. LokPal must always monitor the happiness of farmers in his state.*

66 Create Water Reservoirs

Narada then inquires,"Whether you have created large water reservoirs across your state in all parts? Have you ensured that agriculture in your state is not dependent on rains?"

Building water harvesting systems is extremely important for the long term survival of the state. This is an age old practice to conserve water using large reservoirs to maintain continuity of food production in all types of weather. *Generally, canal's were built from the main rivers or their tributaries along with the ponds to ensure that water is available for drinking or irrigation during Mahabharata era. Small & big water ponds were built all over the country to ensure supply of good water all year round. A complex system of small & large water ponds were constructed to ensure automatic purification of water. This also ensures a high underground water table which in turn makes all wells filled with drinking water.*

Farmers should not be just dependent on Rain water. *Taxes collected by LokPal are used to fund all these water harvesting projects.* Granaries need to be built all over the state along with Water reservoirs and a good system of Canals for appropriate water distribution. *Most granaries are located at least one mile from the nearest water pond. This ensures that granaries are free from all moisture even during the worst rains.*

All ancient cities in the kingdom of Yudhishthira were built with unique water systems to support agriculture. *LokPal has to ensure adequate water supply to all citizens including animals to ensure good health. LokPal must also engage qualified citizen guards to protect these water reservoirs at all times.*

Linking rivers, creating bridges and creating water reservoirs are some of the principal activities of LokPal. LokPal needs to ensure that there is potable drinking water available to all citizens of the state. *Free quality drinking water must be available in all parts of the country. LokPal must also construct free rest areas at regular intervals on all major state highways for the convenience of all citizens. Such facilities must be built with the highest quality highlighting the local architecture and culture. This also promotes local culture & languages. The security of those places must be provided by the state intelligence as well as the secret service of LokPal.* It is the responsibility of LokPal to ensure quality supply of free water and quality food supply to all his citizens.

67 Maintaining Granaries

Narada then inquires,"Whether you have ensured that there are granaries built across your state for your farmers to store their grains and other produce? Do you bestow your farmers with cheap loans at a rate of 1% so that they are never stressed?"

It's usually very difficult for farmers to focus on storage management and financial systems because they are extremely busy in on-field activities. State must provide all help to farmers to store their grains at state granaries without any additional charge. This is the way the state builds their state grain reserves. *LokPal must build large granaries across the length & breadth of the state. Those granaries must be protected by LokPal at all times.*

It's the responsibility of the state to provide them with a system of storage management, financial management and also commercialization assistance for their produce. *State must provide dependable financial assistance to all farmers to protect them from the fluctuation of seasons. The state must also provide a dependable scheme of buying all their produce should there be any seasonal weather changes. LokPal must also provide affordable loans to ensure the financial well being of all farmers.* Low interest rate loans are a big help to the farmers. When a farmer is happy then the state becomes powerful. *Farmers must be provided loans at just 1% of the finance cost of interest and other fees included. LokPal must also create safeguards so that such schemes are not misused by others who pretend to be farmers.*

Granaries must be emptied every three years so that grains don't rot. Excess grains and seeds must be freely distributed every year. *Ideally, granaries must have a rotating six month replenishment period. But each of the granaries must contain a supply of at least three years to provide food security for animals & citizens in the event of natural calamities. All important grains such as wheat, corn, maize, rice and beans must be stocked in those granaries. The focus should be to store locally produced grains because those can be easily stored for a long time. In addition, salt, jaggery and spices must also be stocked for emergency use. LokPal must also make policies for security and distribution of food from granaries.*

68 Organizing Conferences

Narada then inquires,"Whether your kingdom has people experienced in speaking on trade & commerce, agriculture and cow protection? Because people engaged in the profession of speaking on those topics create wealth for themselves and also for others." *This specialized professional speakers based experience sharing is an age-old profession existing from time immemorial.*

The speaking, training and consulting industry is one of the oldest professions in the world. It was even existing 5000 years ago. These professions have created wealth for everyone associated. *Experience creates wealth. LokPal must host conferences and also promote such people engaged in sharing their experiences with their trade communities. Wealth is always in niche specialization. It is the duty of LokPal to create new opportunities for prosperity for his citizens.*

The innovation in Agriculture especially commercialization of agriculture comes from consultants outside the industry. Similarly, innovation in Cow Protection also comes from outside. Cows were the wealth of society because of their being the source of milk and other derived milk products and therefore the protection of cows was the state's responsibility. *People who have experience in trade, agriculture and cow protection must be provided avenues to share their experiences all over the world. Especially, people who have created wealth for themselves must also share their experience through trade and specialized conferences.*

Trade & Commerce was very widespread given the wealth of society. Speakers on Trade and commerce constituted an important segment of society from the beginning of creation. *It is ironic that the European historians don't have any such information because they haven't listened to much older civilizations such as Vedic civilization. The practices of trade have never changed in history, however, tools for conducting trades change as society degrades in values. Many great rishis & munis mentioned in Ramayana & Mahabharata had expertise in trade & commerce also. They would explain through various conferences in those times also.*

State must sponsor a conference in every area of trade and governance to get new ideas in every sphere of statecraft. If possible, LokPal must attend each one or send his trusted aides to each of the conferences. *It is the duty of LokPal to continuously encourage economic development through various means. LokPal is the head of the state and he must know the importance of trade & commerce for peace & prosperity in the society.*

LokPal must organize at least one conference on each of these areas annually:

1. Warfare strategies
2. Weapons
3. Agriculture
4. Education
5. Trade
6. Professions
7. Sanatana Dharma
8. History
9. Environment Conservation
10. City Planning
11. Architecture
12. Clothing

13. Arthashastra
14. Healthcare (based on Ayurveda)
15. Water Conservation
16. Arts & Entertainment
17. Emerging Technology
18. Varnasharama
19. Journalism
20. Spy craft
21. Technology
22. International Diplomacy

When the LokPal ignores promotion of trade & commerce through conferences then his tax collection drops and it directly makes his position weaker than before. *The state becomes weak when the trade & commerce doesn't flourish in the state.*

69   Governing through Panchayat

Narada then inquires,"Whether every village in your Janpad (districts or prefectures in your country) have a committee of five members each that are valiant (experienced in security), intelligent and proficient who work efficiently with one another for the benefit of their people to ensure welfare for all?"

The five members are chosen in following expertise areas

1. Varnashrama expertise
2. Finance skills
3. Security skills
4. Organization skills
5. Deep knowledge in Ramayana & Mahabharata through Parampara

The welfare of villages is considered the topmost priority of a King. Here, a system of efficient management of villages is well defined. This system of management of villages through five prominent village members is currently used in India. *The criteria for selecting the members of Panchayat are: loyalty towards dharma, expertise in at least one area, loyalty towards LokPal, experience in at least one area mentioned above. Collectively, the panchayat serves to provide governance at the grassroots level. Panchayat implements the governance of the LokPal at the local level. It is the most complete government that connects directly with the people. It is the basis of Loktantra.*

Panchayat[41] Raj[42] is the backbone of any state. The state must ensure empowerment of villages to build an internal strength. *All state officials of the LokPal must take the Panchayat into confidence before they implement their plans at the village level. All members of the Panchayat should be paid directly by the state. The members of Panchayat are the retired state officials who have executed similar positions at the state level. No panchayat member must serve for more than two years in that panchayat. Only in an exceptional scenario should a person be elected again for that particular responsibility.*

70   Securing Villages

Narada then inquires, "Whether your villages are as secure as your cities? Have you provided the same quality of security personnel to villages as you have done to cities? Have you ensured that border villages have all facilities as compared to other villages in the Kingdom? Do all those villages, cities and states give you taxes willingly?"

The security of people begins with the security of villages. Each country is divided into districts and those districts into villages. The security of the country begins with the security of villages. *The security of the village is the responsibility of the panchayat. They should seek state help whenever required to provide security to the residents of the village. If a panchayat member is engaged in financial corruption or harassing the village members, then that member and his entire family be asked to leave the village after taking away their properties & all wealth. Furthermore, if a panchayat member is found indulged in serious criminal activities, then that Panchayat member must be given capital punishment. The state must provide the same level of security to villages as it provides to the city.*

The management of Border villages has been particularly stressed here by Narada Muni. Border villages exist in all nation states and the security of those villages depends on the happiness of residents. Those residents need to feel welcome to be part of a powerful state by providing them facilities on a par with the best available in the state. The border villages bear the brunt of enemy action in all situations. *Border villages must have the same level of facilities like any other village in the state. The panchayat of border villages must be made up of retired soldiers.*

LokPal must settle the best soldiers in border villages after their honorable discharge from the state military forces. All villages must be trained in waging a war if a need arises. Border Villages must be given additional preference in recruitment to the state military.

Border village chief gives taxes to the District tax chief who gives taxes to the City Tax chief and who in turn gives taxes to the State tax chief who gives tax to the King. *All border villages must pay the same tax to their district as any other village. State should spend more money on defense in the border villages.* That was the system prevalent in the society. Taxes are an important component of revenue receipts by the states.

There is a formal system of maximum taxation to not exceed 25% of total income of any individual in any calendar year. In lieu of those taxes the King takes complete responsibility for protection from criminals, hostile states and stability of the state. *Any taxation that exceeds 25% of the net household income becomes a burden on the quality of life of a citizen. It also impedes the economic progress of the state.*

When a village is protected, the country is automatically protected. Protection of villages entails protection of its culture, language and administering proper justice to all. *LokPal must ensure that the language spoken in the border villages must be the*

same as that spoken generally in the state. The culture of the border village must be the same as national culture. The administration of border villages must not only be provided by the local panchayat but also the military.

71 Visibility of Security

Narada then inquires, "Whether your key security chiefs take your army in small batches to accessible and inaccessible cities and Villages to destroy, thieves, criminals and looters?"

That's the purpose of taxes. To ensure justice and protection to the last person in any village. *State military units must be visible in all remote villages through regular show of control. Such practices ensure the protection of common citizens from criminals and influence of other enemy states. Security drives economic progress. The best way to ensure security in remote parts is to open military recruitment centers there and also opening sports complexes in those areas.*

Armies, police are not meant to just project state power, they are to be used particularly to provide security to every individual of the state proactively. Here, Narada is particularly inquiring whether your security teams proactively identify and eliminate rogue elements in the state. They have to protect the people proactively. *The retired military officials must be hired to build security infrastructures in remote parts of the state. Yudhishthir Maharaja would regularly recruit his soldiers from all remote parts of the country.*

LokPal must ensure

- State secret service to patrol every village
- Armies to patrol border villages in addition to above
- Heavy artillery must be placed close to border villages in secret locations

LokPal must assure an extremely offensive military aggression to the enemy across the border state. To maintain the security of the border state, LokPal must assure his citizens that the military will take the most offensive attack against the enemy across the entire border. Such fear in the hearts of the enemy protects the border villages.

72   Protecting Women

Narada then inquires, "Whether you keep women satisfied by giving them credible assurances proactively? Do you ensure that women in your kingdom feel fully secured? I hope you do not put blind trust on women? I hope you don't reveal secrets to them while putting blind trust in them."

Women flourish when they feel secure in a state. A king is supposed to build the systems and processes to make them feel secure. *All citizens must be trained to respect every female except wives as mothers irrespective of their age. That is a Vedic system. Boys must be trained from childhood to respect women as mothers. Women must be trained to be chaste & loyal to their families. LokPal must regularly give assurance to women on their security. LokPal must publicly proclaim the capital punishment to those who violate the security of women. Without fear of dharma, women's security becomes weak. (Dharma & law are interchangeable words)*

Also, he needs to protect himself from needless controversies arising out of revealing state secrets to untrusted women. Many enemy states use women to collect state secrets from the King. Herein, Narada cautions Yudhishthira on falling into that trap. *LokPal must never reveal any secrets to anyone but his Guru. LokPal must not trust any visiting women leaders from other countries. Ideally, LokPal must never meet any women alone or in a group without any of his assistants present there.*

Women are protected through

1. Law enforcement
2. Family care, and
3. Respect

All the above are attained through strict knowledge of dharma being given to every citizen. *Yudhishthir himself practiced this, and therefore, he was trusted by all his citizens.*

73   Availability during Crisis

Narada then inquires, "Whether you indulge yourself in personal enjoyment or even sleep even after hearing bad news? You may be even meditating on possible solutions but due to fear of facing the issue directly you keep procrastinating while enjoying it with your loved ones."

Procrastination is the biggest enemy of the LokPal when facing a critical issue. Also, personal enjoyment of a king has to be controlled so that the normal functions of the state continue. *LokPal must never procrastinate any decision on any issue. Also, LokPal must immediately leave any entertainment or sleep when he hears of a crisis. Failure to do so results in loss of respect in the eyes of ministers & important officials.*

The LokPal needs to be available to his subjects at all times during a crisis. The best way to do this is to write the description of the crisis in a simple manner for self understanding. *LokPal must never worry about his sleep or personal rest when he hears of any crisis in his state. All his ministers & officials automatically follow the conduct of LokPal because they look up to him for inspiration & guidance. LokPal must use logic & reasoning to break down all aspects of the crisis to understand the problem. Then he should consult with his officials & ministers for further analysis & solutions.*

Once the problem has been defined then the following four approaches need to be used

1. Identifying the actors in the crisis
2. Identifying Roles and importance of each of the actors
3. Playing all scenarios from best to worst

4. Discussing with a trusted advisor before choosing one scenario

5. Immediate action against the core issue first before attending the symptoms of the issue

Decisiveness of a LokPal brings him / her popularity in the public eye. *Short-term relief for the symptoms of the problems must be immediately initiated. At the same time, a long-term solution for the main problem needs to be initiated. If any enemy is behind such a problem then the military action must be immediately taken against the enemy.*

74 Managing Personal Time

Narada then inquires, "Whether you sleep well during the second two phases of a night, and then get up early during the last phase to meditate on dharma and Artha (economics)?"

A LokPal needs to lead a very regulated life even when sleeping and waking up. Usually as per science the night is divided into four separate sections. The first section is usually meant for enjoyment and the next two sections for total rest, while the fourth section is reserved for dharma and Artha for the King. When the king regulates his life like this, then he becomes successful. *The entire personal staff of LokPal must ensure that LokPal always gets proper rest. When the LokPal is not properly rested, he might make wrong decisions that may hurt the security of the state in the long run.*

LokPal must take adequate rest as required by his body. *LokPal must not be disturbed from his periodic rest or vacation unless a severe crisis is faced by the state. Ministers & Officials must be empowered to take important decisions to resolve any crisis.*

Any lack of rest will result in lack of attention. In addition, the LokPal must engage in physical activities to maintain good health. *The Guru of LokPal must monitor the spiritual health of*

LokPal to advise him on a regular basis. When the LokPal stops waking up early in the morning for his spiritual activities, then that should also become a cause for concern for the Guru. When the economic growth slows down then it should become a cause of concern for the Minister who is in charge of finance & taxation. When LokPal is indifferent to the growing military prowess of the enemy, then the council of ministers must first give a warning to the LokPal and then if the situation needs, must also replace the LokPal.

75   Elegant Dress and Hygiene

Narada then inquires,"Whether you ensure to take care of all desires and requests of your visitors and subjects early in the morning? Do you meet your ministers early in the morning after dressing up properly to understand the happenings in your state every morning? "

It is important for the King to wake up early to meet all people who come to meet him or come to him with special requests. But before that he needs to meet his ministers to get full information on his state. *After receiving the full report about the health of the state, LokPal must order all his ministers to carry out the important tasks as needed. Then, LokPal must take his breakfast before attending any visitors. Then, LokPal must dress properly before meeting any visitor. A special grooming team must help LokPal dress up for all public appearances. The clothes worn by LokPal must carry all symbols of power, colors of his preference, jewellery as per taste and also colors as per his astrological charts. All symbols of state power must be visible when the LokPal meets his guests. All important ministers must be in full attendance before LokPal meets ambassadors of different states. Only military commanders must meet the ambassadors of enemy states.*

LokPal must meet all his important secretaries and ministers in the early morning to take stock of the state. By late morning, all important decisions must be announced to the public. *LokPal must set a protocol to attend visitors. All visitors must be fully checked about their credentials and a defined purpose of visit before they are presented in front of LokPal. LokPal must announce all important policy decisions before his noon sandhya (prayers at noon).*

All decisions must be announced between 11 am and 12 noon by executive order of the LokPal. *LokPal must be in attendance when his council of ministers announce important decisions by the LokPal. All announcements in the state must be announced on behalf of LokPal. Then, the officials need to be sent in every part of the state to personally explain all policy decisions.*

76 Uniforms of Bodyguards

Narada then inquires, "Whether well trained soldiers with open swords protect you from all sides especially wearing red uniforms?"

Red Uniforms are particularly suggested here for personal guards of the king. Also, it is advised for them to be completely ready at all times. *Red color is especially advised because it stands out. Also, it is the color of passion and aggression. LokPal carries the authority of waging a war and also maintaining dharma in his state, therefore, his personal bodyguards must be equipped with all the latest weapons as well as techniques to protect LokPal. The numbers of personal bodyguards & weapons & techniques used must never be revealed to the public. The personal bodyguards of LokPal must always be ready to use military force to protect his life. No bodyguard must have ever talked against dharma.*

LokPal should have his personal security guards equipped with

- Cavalry
- Heavy artillery
- All types of vehicles including boat, land and air
- Ambulances with all medical specialties on standby

The personal security of the LokPal must be exclusively loyal to him and must not mix with regular soldiers of the state. *The guards must be chosen from the most battle worthy soldiers. They must be kept on rotation basis so that they are rewarded from being posted as personal bodyguards. All of them must have deep love and devotion for the LokPal. The intelligence and the secret service of the*

LokPal must always ensure that every single bodyguard is loyal to LokPal during the times of his deployment.

Personal security of the LokPal must be drawn from State forces but maintained separately from state forces. *The bodyguards must be given separate training to protect the LokPal. Because personal protection is a specialized task. The bodyguards must ensure that no one comes even close to LokPal unless approved by the secret service. Even ministers & officials must be made to follow the same protocol.*

77   Punishment Policy

Narada then inquires,"Whether you screen people before you meet them? Do you behave appropriately towards people after knowing about them through proper screening? Do you have separate standards for providing justice to criminals (Yamraj[43]) and rewards to respectful people (Dharmaraj[44]) ? Do you ensure that criminals receive appropriate punishment and respectable people receive appropriate rewards?"

A standard screening process needs to be set up for a king to ensure that King doesn't meet random people. Because one of the main purposes of a king is to provide justice. Criminals need to be given the hardest punishment so that it dissuades them from committing any criminal acts. *Not the same punishment needs to be given to criminals and civil offenders. LokPal must create a system of gradation of punishment so that excessive punishment is not given to anyone.*

Four categories of punishment for four categories of people

- Teachers should be punished through reprimands
- Administrators through taking away their land
- Traders through financial penalties
- Thieves & other criminals through physical punishment

Rewards and Punishment are the topics of Dharma. LokPal is supposed to uphold dharma at all times. Without fear of punishment, the state becomes ungovernable. Capital punishment is the sole prerogative of LokPal. LokPal must never delegate such powers to anyone especially large committees or jury. When LokPal delegates such responsibility to others, then the state becomes lawless. All enemy spies must be subject to capital punishment unless the secret service of the LokPal wants to use them for their purpose. All criminals who have killed any other human must be subject to capital punishment unless the officials carefully analyze the reasons for such crime to be accidental. Such criminals must be relocated to undisclosed locations away from their families. *For additional details, people can consult important treatises on justice in Manusmriti or Ramayana or Mahabharata.*

78   Maintaining Personal Health

Narada then inquires, "Whether you ensure that you take care of your body through medicines and special meals? Do you ensure that you remove your mental stress through Satsang (congregational chanting) along with elderly people?"

Ayurvedic Medicines and Congregational chanting of the Holy name are traditionally considered important to maintain the total health of the LokPal. *LokPal's diet should be very special and should contain rare grains & vegetables. LokPal must also consume special oils as well as spices. Ayurvedic doctors must always administer special medicines to LokPal to ensure that LokPal is alert at all times. The personal cooks of LokPal must. be trained to prepare exclusive meals for him at all times. LokPal's personal diet must never be revealed to the public as well as his important ministers and officials. LokPal must himself ensure that his diet is optimum. If a LokPal cannot take care of his own health, then he is not qualified to rule the state.*

Maintaining a special diet is important for a LokPal to ensure optimum health. All mental challenges must be resolved through Kirtana and hearing discourses on Bhagavad Gita. *LokPal must always be interested in Yog because his mental well-being is as important as his physical well-being. Chanting the names of Hari is a sure way to remove mental stress. If a LokPal doesn't engage in such Yog solutions, then he becomes unqualified to rule the state.*

79 Keeping Good Personal Doctors

Narada then inquires, "Whether your doctors are well versed in all eight parts of medical science? Whether your doctors are capable, your well wisher and they love you as a person? Whether your doctors are always sincerely busy taking care of your body and keeping you healthy?"

The Ayurveda describes eight different sections of medical science dealing with a human body. *Ayurveda and Sushruta Samhita are the original guide books on medicine. Every doctor must be trained on those to ensure excellence in medical practices. The personal doctors of LokPal must not only be expert in advising ayurvedic diet but also be experts in medical solutions to ensure optimum physical health of LokPal.*

Personal doctors of LokPal must be expert in analyzing:

1. नाड़ी Nerves (can also refer to Pran Vayu flow)
2. मल Excreta
3. मूत्र Urinary
4. जिह्वा Tongue
5. नेत्र Eyes
6. रूप Body Skin
7. शब्द Vocal Chords
8. स्पर्श Touch

The LokPal's doctors need to be an expert in all those and take strict care of the body of the king appropriately in all those categories. *LokPal must be trained in Yog asanas to ensure an optimum flow of pran through Nadis. If a LokPal doesn't engage in such preventative measures then the ministers automatically deem such LokPal as irresponsible. Personal health of the LokPal is the responsibility of the LokPal.*

The personal doctors must be part of the internal security team of the LokPal because they are as important as the physical security of the LokPal. *A large group of doctors of all specialties must always accompany LokPal. Whenever a LokPal travels, then these doctors must attend to the care of LokPal. However, these doctors must also render service to citizens in general when the LokPal is not traveling. These services to all citizens must always be free of any charge.*

80   Addressing Grievances

Narada then inquires, "Whether you behave arrogantly towards those petitioners who approach you for the first time or second time to seek their stopped wages? I hope you avoid covetousness, attachment and pride towards those seekers. I also hope that you don't ignore those people who come to you with some financial hope."

A LokPal needs to be humble with all types of seekers to him. Especially those seekers who have a genuine grievance against the state. When any of the state employees have been penalized through stoppage of their salaries, LokPal should carefully analyze their case and provide necessary instructions to his officials to ensure that undue hardship is not caused to the families of such petitioners. *LokPal's officials & employees must be free from any accusation of nepotism because it directly affects the reputation of LokPal. LokPal must also ensure that any stoppage of salary to any of his employees was the outcome from a detailed investigation.*

Arthi - First time seekers must be patiently heard by the LokPal. They must be provided state help even if the complaint is trivial. No one should go back empty handed when they visit the LokPal. *Their complaints must be favorably discharged after obtaining a written assurance of corrective behavior.*

Pratyarthi - the second or third time seekers must also be heard and given token acknowledgement but no benefits. *The repeat offenders must face punishment which must be commensurate with the repeat offense. However, if LokPal finds out that the enemy state was involved in misleading his employee, then that employee must be removed from all state employment.*

LokPal must never deny financial assistance to anyone who approaches him for help. *LokPal must use state institutions to deliver financial aid after verifying the credentials of the seeker. Failure to respond results in loss of trust amongst his own supporters.* LokPal must never mock the seeker on account of his position and power. LokPal must always remain humble while addressing the needs of the seeker.

81 Protecting loyal subjects

Narada then inquires,"Whether you stop the salaries of your dependents out of covetousness, greed, overconfidence and bad attachment? Ensure you do not stop their salaries for which they are dependent on you."

King needs to ensure that people who are trusting him with a regular income should receive what they trusted him for. Trust in the LokPal is extremely important for the citizens. LokPal must never break the trust of those who are dependent on him. *For complex scenarios, LokPal must send his senior most ministers to meet the concerned state employees to assure them of justice. His ministers must convey the underlying decisions for the action. After explaining the reasons and demanding corrective actions, LokPal must resume their salaries.*

Salaries of any state dependent must never be stopped without a prior show cause notice. Stopping the salary for any reason reduces the loss of confidence in the LokPal. *LokPal must always remain free from ill will, greed, pride, attachment and overconfidence while administering any decision especially against any loyal subjects. LokPal must never try to divide his loyal subjects by favoring one over the other. Loyal subjects must always be treated with respect and honor for their past service.*

LokPal must ensure that a public notice must be given before stopping anyone's salary on the following grounds

- Treason to state
- Theft of state resources

LokPal must regularly honor and reward loyalty through his actions. The best way to do that is to institutionalize the reward system. Every state subject must be aware of criteria for promotion as well as demotion. Three favorable outcomes must be criteria for promotion whereas three unfavorable actions must be a criteria for demotion. Any action against dharma or state must be considered for the highest possible punishment. *By making such policies for reward & punishment public, LokPal remains above any type of accusation.*

82 Protecting Important Citizens

Narada then inquires, "Whether your citizens don't assemble together to organize protests against you? Do you ensure that your enemies haven't bribed them to oppose you?"

Many enemies want to ensure the downfall of a good king. A good king is the biggest threat for dishonest people. Fake protests are usually organized to trouble the efforts of the King. King must use his secret services to ensure that he knows about the protestors and their sponsors to take appropriate action. *LokPal's secret service must always monitor the movement of the enemy's disinformation sources in the society. All media and influential people in the state must be subject to the state policies. LokPal must always keep in touch with important opinion makers and rich businessmen in his state. When LokPal's secret service identifies the source for a potential enemy financed rebellion against the LokPal, they should automatically take an action against that source even without the knowledge of LokPal. LokPal must always be above any type of suspicion of authoritarianism.*

"Action determines the success of the lokPal."

When an enemy is able to influence the citizens through any type of allurement, then that is a danger to the security of the state. *LokPal must be willing & capable to wage a war against that enemy state. LokPal must not tolerate such actions of the enemy. Failure to wage a war against the enemy results in lack of popularity of the LokPal.*

LokPal must immediately attack the enemy state with destructive weapons to completely destroy the capacity of the enemy to wage a war. Then the LokPal must destroy all the spies of enemies in his own country. *All enemy spies must be given capital punishment for endangering the security of the state.*

83 Conclusively defeating enemies

Narada then inquires,"Whether your enemy who was defeated by you by force but not killed began to trouble you again? Does your defeated enemy have assembled good advisors and a stronger military than you, who have again begun to challenge your authority? Have you taken strong action against such an enemy?"

The LokPal needs to ensure military and advisory superiority over his enemies at all times. Never letting the guard down is the sign of successful LokPal. There should be dedicated departments for those types of specific enemies. *The defeated enemy must always be monitored and continuously kept weak until there is a visible change in behavior for a minimum period of ten years. LokPal's military and secret service must completely control all aspects of the defeated enemy until they accept the rule of dharma.*

Defeating the enemy for good is the ultimate objective of LokPal. *LokPal must never show any leniency towards any enemy. LokPal must constantly monitor the quality of advisors, state of military and political leadership of the enemy.*

The enemies' financial resources, military resources must be completely destroyed without any mercy so that even two generations of enemies are not able to muster enough courage to stand up to the state. *Such decisive actions against the enemy protects the state of the LokPal. Ideally, LokPal must try to merge all the lands of the enemy into his own state. There should be no enemy state for at least 800 miles from the immediate borders of the state of LokPal. During Yudhishthir's rule, there were no enemy states within 800 mile distance in the north and west of Hastinapur.*

84   Gaining Loyalty of Bhupal

Narada then inquires,"Whether all your important controllers of parts of your state (Bhupal) controllers love you unquestionably? Are they willing to sacrifice their life for you after receiving due respect and benefit from you? "

Bhupal[45] are the most important constituents for the LokPal. LokPal must try his best to win their love and in case he can't. He should remove them from those positions. *Bhupal or maintainer of five districts or 125 villages is the most important constituent of LokPal's administration. Every Bhupal must be able to gain the audience of LokPal on a monthly basis. Bhupal's must always be checked on their loyalty towards LokPal. If Bhupal is not competent, then he must be replaced after due diligence by the ministers, Guru of LokPal and also the suggestions of the secret service of LokPal. Bhupal must also cultivate the qualities needed to be considered for the position of LokPal if the need arises. Generally, Bhupals become the LokPal for the entire country.*

LokPals can have many Bhupal under him. Each janpad or district has a Bhupal who has multiple Panchayat Pradhan under them. LokPal needs to ensure that every Bhupal is able to attract village sarpanch to willingly pay taxes to him. Each Bhupal must also deposit those taxes to the state treasury. *Bhupal carries the same responsibility like the LokPal at a local level of governance. They also lead the wars against enemy states should there be a need for such involvement. Bhupal is also a military soldier. Bhupal needs to follow the same routine like the LokPal to gain trust of everyone in his region of responsibility on behalf of LokPal. If Bhupal is proud, arrogant and cruel, then it automatically brings disrepute to the LokPal. If Bhupal delays deposit of taxes in national treasury, then LokPal must immediately replace him. If Bhupal disregards the instructions of LokPal for any reason, then he must be imprisoned for working against the state.*

In order to gain respect of Bhupal, Lokpal must

- Be an expert in Vedic scriptures
- Have a strong moral and spiritual character
- Be an expert on Mahabharata and Ramayana
- Must have a very strong tax collection department
- Must have strong vigilance and secret service
- Must have a very strong military

Power brings respect from all Bhupals to LokPal. *LokPal must regularly cultivate all Bhupals to ensure that they provide the best governance in their regions. The same standards of conduct that apply to LokPal also apply to Bhupal. In today's parlance you can assume them to be the Governors of various provinces in your country. Bhupal's region should never be changed because of his intrinsic connections to the roots of that land. However, they can assist LokPal whenever there is a need.*

85   Respect for Knowledge

Narada then inquires,"Whether you respect all categories of knowledge as per the quality of those knowledge? Do you maintain sincere respect for saintly people, thinkers, educators and the intelligentsia? Do you serve such people? Such behavior for educated people and knowledge itself is very beneficial for you. Do you ensure that you financially reward them appropriately through state resources? Because by honoring such saintly people you will attain heaven and freedom from the repeated cycle of birth and death."

A LokPal who has no respect for the culture of Knowledge and teachers of that wisdom is lost in his endeavor. Respect for Knowledge and preachers of that knowledge is required to create a culture of science in a state. *The LokPal who doesn't value knowledge is not fit to remain in office. Knowledge comes from Vedas and Vedic histories. The LokPal must make a conscious endeavor to continue refreshing his knowledge through regular hearing from advanced seekers and seers of truth. Therefore, the morning time for a LokPal must be reserved for interacting with great personalities whose life revolves around Yog. LokPal must always be eager to serve them and humbly ask them questions to receive the boon of knowledge. This attitude of LokPal makes him dear to all including his enemies.*

A LokPal must show his respect for Knowledge by

- Opening new libraries
- Respecting teachers and intelligentsia
- Encouraging writers & thinkers whose heart is dedicated to Vedas
- Hosting saintly vedic teachers at home regularly

- Organizing conferences on Vedas, Ramayana and Mahabharata

When a LokPal disrespects a saintly vedic teacher, he brings ruination to himself and his state. *LokPal must never introduce politics between the seers of truth. By doing so, LokPal opens his own pathway to ruination. LokPal must always consult his Guru on the matters related to saintly people and follow his advice sincerely.*

LokPal must support the different paths of saintly people knowing well that they are ultimately contributing to the same path of Brahman. The same absolute truth is seen differently by different seekers owing to their own advancement in their seeking. However, LokPal must also search for those seekers who see the ultimate purpose behind all different paths of seekers. Those seekers must be given important positions of Acharyas to guide the whole society. By cultivating a culture of knowledge in his state, LokPal brings peace, harmony and happiness to all.

86 Following Dharma

Narada then inquires, "Your ancestor kings have followed the three Veda (Rig, Sam, Yajur Veda) and dharma that is ordained by those scriptures. Are you always working towards maintaining similar standards as your ancestors did? Do you engage in Karma according to dharma and you are mindfully engaged in it?"

Dharma is the essence of good governance. A king needs to protect dharma at all times. It is the purpose, ways, means and results of all efforts of a king. If the dharma is protected, then it is a complete success for citizens and kings. It ensures complete happiness for everyone. *Yudhishthir had an illustrious family history of powerful Kings. Narada is reminding him of his background. Narada also wants to ensure that Yudhishthir knows that and he would do everything to uphold the virtues of his ancestors. Narada reminds him that his ancestors followed the dharma mentioned in the three Vedas. The three Vedas talk about Dharma in three different modes - Mode of Goodness (Sattva Guna), Mode of Passion (Rajo Guna) and Mode of Ignorance (Tamo Guna).*

A Lokpal must be the biggest supporter of Vedic education and Culture. *LokPal needs to act on Dharmic principles. Those Dharmic principles are the laws of the state. These Dharmic principles were given to humanity by Manu, the son of Brahma. Later, all incarnations of Vishnu come to reinstate those principles for the benefit of common people. LokPal rules the state for this Dharma propounded by Vedas. From Dharma comes Artha (economic development), and then, this Artha has to be used again back in the service of Dharma. LokPal follows this cycle to ensure peace & prosperity of everyone in his state. Therefore, LokPal is directly the custodian of Dharma in his state.*

LokPal must follow the teachings from Ramayana[46] and Mahabharata in managing his state to protect the dharma of all his citizens. *The karma of the LokPal must be according to Dharma. It is the Karma of LokPal that sets the standard of Dharma in his state. When LokPal falls from the path of previous LokPals who followed dharma in their lives, then automatically, he loses the right to rule his state. Therefore, LokPal must dedicate his life to uphold dharma. That makes LokPal the most powerful leader.*

87 Nurturing Teachers

Narada then inquires, "Whether important Vedic teachers eat tasty and healthy meals in front of your eyes? Do you ensure that they receive good financial gifts after eating a healthy meal?"

To properly greet the Vedic teachers, they need to be fed healthy meals right in front of the king's eyes. This ensures a personal connection with those intelligentsia. *It is the duty of LokPal to feed all saintly teachers and seers personally with the best quality food and non-alcoholic drinks. LokPal must also ensure that all temples in his state serve quality meals to an area at least 50 kms radius from every temple. Not only should the LokPal make good food arrangements for all seers, sages, Purohit (vedic priests) and other saintly people in his state but also provide good quality kitchen & free food for everyone visiting the temples. Temples are the best places for removing the problems of hunger & shelter in the society. After feeding them, LokPal must also give valuable gifts for their sustenance. When seers & sages are happy, they bless the society by sharing their knowledge.*

A LokPal must invite saintly people at home and feed them with sanctified food. He should respectfully offer meals and not only serve saintly people with his own hands but also engage his own wife and children in serving those saintly people. After serving them meals he should offer them clothes and gifts before they leave the home. *LokPal must also provide special gifts such as land & jewelry on special occasions like Guru Purnima, Diwali and or any other state celebration on behalf of the state. The current models of governance work against the spiritual interests of the society.*

A personal service by LokPal is the most desirable quality that brings him popularity. *LokPal must also pay good salaries to all saintly seers in the state so that they are not forced to find employment anywhere else. Yudhishthir used to follow this instruction of Narada Muni very sincerely. He maintained almost 88000 sages in his palace, the rest were employed by temples supported by his state. He gave them prominent positions in his assembly house on par with ministers in his cabinet.*

88   Dharmic Ceremonies

Narada then inquires,"Whether you sincerely follow and try to perform Vajpayee and Pundrik Yagya completely after duly controlling your mind? Do you perform these sacrifices after duly controlling your mind?"

These specific procedures are particularly mentioned for the king to appropriately serve dharma in his state. If the King follows such procedures then it bodes well for all citizens of that country. *Vajpayee Yagya honors those sages who repeat stories from Puranas. Pundrak Yagya honors Hari. Both of these Yagyas celebrate the exalted position of Vyasadeva in the society. It is essential that LokPal controls his mind through Yog before he participates in such ceremonies.*

Vedic ceremonies bring

- Good fortune
- Auspiciousness
- Mental strength
- Cooperation of Deva
- Guidance of Vedic experts
- Lessons from past successful LokPal
- Love for Krishna and Ram

The world's foremost LokPals are two - Krishna and Ram. Most people become successful LokPal when they worship Ram. The ideal dream of any LokPal should be to establish Ram Rajya. *Ram Rajya is the golden standard of governance as covered in detail in this book. In Ram Rajya, the complete sustainable governance is practiced for complete perfection of humanity. There is no exploitation, no sickness, people have long lives, there is no unemployment and there is always a victory in any war.*

All Yagya are performed to please Ram and Krishna. Another name for Ram and Krishna is Hari. All activities performed for Hari are called Yajna or Yagya. In this age the best way to perform Yajna or Yagya is to perform Harinam (name of Hari) Yagya. Every LokPal should popularize the street chanting of Hari in every town and village. *LokPal's management of the state is for the purpose of Yagya or pleasing devatas. All leaders of the world must emulate the example of Yudhishthir. Because there is a one world government which is the government of devatas.*

The mantra for bringing social peace and harmony is:

Hare Rama Hare Rama Rama Rama Hare Hare

Hare Krishna Hare Krishna Krishna Krishna Hare Hare

These sixteen names of Hari, when chanted by a large group of people in the country of any LokPal brings peace, prosperity and wealth. That is the biggest publicly known secret. This mantra reestablishes Sanatana Dharma in any land it is practiced. This mantra brings fame to LokPal. *LokPal must also participate in such events in his state. By participating in such events, LokPal becomes more endearing to his citizens.*

89 Respect Sacred People and Places

Narada then inquires, "Whether you offer your respectful obeisances or greetings to your community brothers, teachers, elderly, devata, tapasvi (a strict observer of a spiritual practice), Chaitya Vriksh (sacred trees such as peepal), and merciful teachers?"

It's important for the LokPal to be respectful to a wide variety of citizens and other spiritual practices especially connected to Dharma. *When LokPal honors others without any expectation of reciprocation, then he gets honored more by his citizens.*

It is the duty of every LokPal to establish or create sacred places in the country. Every LokPal should establish Harinam centers in every town and village. He should encourage Panchayat to chant and all Bhupal to ensure that every village or janpad should be chanting this mantra. *LokPal must inaugurate more places than the previous LokPal to add to the legacy. By creating & maintaining such places, LokPal gets permanently etched in the good memories of his citizens.*

Groups of five - a structure for governance:

- Five important people make a panchayat for every village, their head is Panch Pradhan
- Five villages is considered a city
- Five cities make up a Janpad
- Each Janpad has a Bhupal
- Five Janpads create a province
- Five provinces have a Bhupal Pradhan
- Five bhupal Pradhan come under Minister

- There are many ministers under a LokPal

This is how a country is managed by the LokPal. The smallest unit of governance is the village. This model of governance creates major economic activity in the villages due to which the cities don't get crowded. This model of governance not only creates a scale of development but also retains the high quality of life for all citizens. *LokPal must create systems for accountability at each level which must be monitored by his secret service, intelligence and vigilance departments.*

90 Understanding Citizens

Narada then inquires, "Whether you increase sadness or anger in people? I hope you have someone near you always standing with auspicious items."

It's important for the King to have a pleasing personality. Harsh words don't help for heads of State. Lots of work needs to be completed ahead of their meeting with any individual. *LokPal must always extract a pleasing response from his citizens. In the event he finds out that people are not happy, he should constitute a team to understand the core reasons for dissatisfaction. After carefully analyzing the root cause of dissatisfaction, LokPal should immediately take short term action against the errant officials. Then, he should simultaneously take long term corrective actions so that such situations don't arise.*

After this Narada takes a pause and again verifies from Yudhishthira whether he follows all that has so far been inquired by him.

This type of dharma friendly thought process and actions will help him to achieve success in managing his kingdom. Any head of state who follows this advice will always be able to keep his state out of trouble. That King can easily win the entire planet and live peacefully along with his kingdom.

Narada wants LokPal to acknowledge his teachings first. He asks whether his population follows this congregational chanting of Mantra which helps reduce sadness and anger in people. Mantra is the best way to make people happy. *LokPal must set an example for his citizens through his actions.*

Narada, the Guru of all Statesmen

91   Narada Checks on LokPal

Narada then assures Yudhishthira ,"Whatever has been told by you, is your intelligence, thought process and behavior according to that? This type of Dharmic Intelligence and behavior will increase your life, popularity and will help you to properly execute your dharma, economics and all your material desires."

It is the duty of a teacher to confirm whether the student has learnt properly. Once the student confirms then further instructions can be given. *Yudhishthir confirms that he has been performing his duties as LokPal as per the instructions given by Narada. Yudhishthir has been the greatest emperor the world has ever seen.*

92   Narada's Assurance

Narada then assures Yudhishthira ,"One who acts with such intelligence , his state never falls into trouble. That LokPal wins the entire earth and progresses daily."

After LokPal confirms, Narada blesses the LokPal that he will win the entire earth for Hari and his people will progress on spiritual and material paths. *Yudhishthir did conquer the entire world by following the instructions of Narada. His rule was marked with peace, prosperity and tremendous growth of dharma.*

The LokPal needs to cultivate his intelligence through

- Harinam
- Sanatana dharma
- Preaching of Vedic culture

LokPal actually transcends even mind, intelligence and false ego by following Yog practices. Yog actually sharpens intelligence. LokPal must act against all challenges after due diligence. Also, LokPal must take lessons from histories of Puranas and then act thoughtfully to ensure effective governance to all his citizens.

93   Intellectual Property

Narada then inquires, "Whether your corrupt ministers have acquired the wealth of an intelligent Brahmin by accusing him for stealing and cheating? And then they also give that Brahmin life sentence?"

It's important to control all officials of the state. When officials are not controlled they work directly against the LokPal. The LokPal must control his officials to never criticize the Vedic saintly people in his State. *Brahmins bring innovation through their intellect. Kshatriyas bring innovation in governance & military. Vaishya creates wealth through innovation. Shudra brings innovation in service. However, the legal protection for their respective innovation is protected by the LokPal. LokPal must create a system of regulation by which such intellectual property is protected so that people are encouraged to innovate more. LokPal must not spare anyone including his ministers who steal such intellectual property.*

Instructions to Officials:

- Never criticize Vedic saintly people
- Provide monthly stipend to every Vedic saintly person
- Protect temples of Sanatana Dharma
- Protect the officials who protect Sanatana Dharma

- Protect all people who chant Harinam because those people are the biggest asset to LokPal
- Make Bhagavad Gita as the official book of the state

Bhagavad Gita clarifies the difference between dharma and adharma. It provides LokPal with the standards for making effective decisions. *LokPal must not even spare priests, seers and even teachers who plagiarize the intellectual property of anyone else. Failure to do so will hamper economic progress in his state.*

94 Preventing Corruption in Prisons

Narada then inquires,"Whether a thief who was caught red handed by guards and was caught with the stolen goods is not let free through financial bribes?"

Here Narada inquires about the state of anti-corruption operations of LokPal. LokPal must create campaigns at regular intervals to root out corrupt officials and their cronies. Bribery of any sort must be banned by the state. The best way to remove corruption is to put a small fee for every service performed by the state. That fee needs to be used for the welfare of officials. The fees need to be a standard count of ten lowest denominations of currency. For example, the fees for any service in the USA should be 10 cents and it can go up to 10 dollars for any form. Same for any other state in the world. Any citizen should be able to afford that service fee. *LokPal must institute a very strong penal system for anti-corruption actions. All citizens must be aware of severe punishment ordained for those engaging in or promoting corruption at any level of governance.*

A vigilance department helps LokPal to monitor the activities of every official. That vigilance department should be able to punish that official accused of corruption through

- Suspension from service
- Penalty - should be one year salary for every act
- One year tough imprisonment
- Death penalty for severe corruption and harassment

95   Trusting Newly Rich People

Narada then inquires, "Whether your ministers don't suspect newly rich people? Whether your ministers don't suspect a rich person or a newly rich person based on mere hearsay or allegation? Whether your ministers dont assume that the newly rich person may have obtained his wealth through theft or other criminal means? Whether your ministers suspect a poor man becoming rich suddenly?"

The newly rich people run the economy of the state. They need to be respected. The country's economy runs on new ideas and new business ventures. The LokPal must evaluate whether that new idea brings better quality of life to the citizens of his state. *LokPal must never envy rich people who have obtained their wealth through their hard work and have paid their taxes to the state treasury. LokPal must also ensure that such wealth has not rendered others poorer. Wealth creation must not be at the cost of creation of poverty elsewhere. LokPal must immediately target unfair trading practices that create poverty somewhere else.* That should be the only criteria to give freedom to all citizens to create financial well-being for themselves.

Newly rich

- Must be protected by LokPal
- Must be given financial rewards such as low taxes
- Must be rewarded socially with a State title
- Must be given all help by State officials
- Must be encouraged to open Education facilities
- Must be encouraged to propagate Harinam Sankirtana

Wealthy citizens must be protected from envious ministers & officials who may act against such citizens through state policies and taxation policies. The standard 25% taxation must not be changed for anyone at any time. *If anyone is found misusing the tax code, then those should be severely punished through the civilian laws. LokPal must train his ministers & officials to celebrate newly rich people in his state. Those citizens must be honored by the state for creating prosperity for themselves and others in the state. LokPal must award such wealth creators in his state.*

96 Fourteen Faults to overcome

Narada then inquires,"Whether you don't have 14 Doshi or faults?

1. नास्तिकता
2. झूठ
3. क्रोध
4. प्रमाद
5. दीर्घसूत्रता
6. ज्ञानियों का संग ना करना
7. आलस्य
8. पाँचों इंद्रियों के विषयों में आसक्ति
9. प्रजाजनों पर अकेले ही विचार करना
10. अर्थशास्त्रों को ना जानने वाले मूर्खों के साथ विचार विमर्श
11. निश्चित कार्यों के आरम्भ करने में विलम्ब या टाल-मेल
12. गुप्त मंत्रणा को सुरक्षित नही रखना
13. माँगलिक उत्सव न करना
14. एक साथ सभी शत्रुओं पर आक्रमण कर देना

Next Narada checks from LokPal Yudhishthira, whether he has ever been introspective if he has 14 faults that can hinder his service to his kingdom. Also, whether he has transcended these fourteen faults. Because even if they have successfully begotten a state, these fourteen qualities destroy the LokPal.

The fourteen qualities that LokPal should avoid are:

1. Atheism (not following Vedic instructions, Rejecting the science of Soul)
2. Lying
3. Anger
4. Mental illness
5. Procrastination
6. Avoiding association of educated and wise people
7. Laziness
8. Sense Gratification with five senses
9. Taking unilateral decision without consulting others
10. Taking consultation of people not well versed in Arthashastra
11. Delaying necessary decisions and activities necessary for the wellbeing of decisions
12. Not keeping secure secret counsel by advisors
13. Not organizing auspicious festivals for citizens
14. Attacking all enemies at once

Avoiding these fourteen shortcomings, a LokPal becomes endeared to his subjects and population. LokPal should also add a group of ministers for all of the above 14 areas of governance to ensure that there is no loose end. *Not only LokPal must avoid these fourteen faults but also his Bhupals and other ministers in his state. LokPal must train all officials also to avoid these fourteen faults.*

97   Quality Benchmarks

Narada then inquires,"Whether your vedas are successful? Whether your wealth is successful? Whether your women are successful? Whether your scriptural knowledge is successful?"

LokPal must introspect whether

- His knowledge is out to good use
- His wealth is put to good use
- His women are producing good children and also educating them in Sanatana dharma
- His scriptural knowledge is put to good use

Knowledge is put to good use when there is happiness and prosperity for all. Wealth is out to good use when it produces more wealth. Women are put to good use when children are happy. Scriptural knowledge is put to good use when there is happiness all around. *LokPal must carefully evaluate his knowledge, wealth, women and Yog knowledge on the standards of Dharma.*

LokPal should ensure

- That new educational institutions are created regularly
- New Financial institutions are created periodically in his state
- Women welfare schemes are launched periodically
- More institutions of Vedic learning are opened periodically

Failure to spread dharma leads automatically to anarchy in the state. Anarchy comes when adharma is prominent in the society. LokPal must be an introspective leader and his actions must speak louder than his words.

98   Important Questions

Yudhishthira then inquires,"How can I measure whether my Vedas are successful? How can I measure whether my wealth is successful? How can I measure whether my women are successful? How can I measure whether my scriptural knowledge is successful?

LokPal Yudhishthira asks the question back to Narada,

1. How can I make Vedas Successful?
2. What is the barometer to measure the success of my wealth?
3. What is the measure of success of my women?
4. How is Spiritual scriptural knowledge successful?

LokPal asks pertinent questions from Narada. Intelligent questions engage the teacher more. These questions will help a statesman to out appropriate policies for all sections of society. *LokPal must have a very analytical mind. Here, Yudhishthir shows that he was attentive to Narada's instructions. Guru gives instructions by asking questions. These questions were very interesting to Yudhishthir, because they gave him a checklist on governance.*

99   Success Formula

Narada then answers, "Fire sacrifice makes Vedas successful, Charity and Utility makes wealth successful, Chastity and Sons make women successful, Modesty and Good Behavior makes Scriptural knowledge successful."

LokPal must ensure that Japa becomes the most common method of Yagya. And all the officials of the state support LokPal's initiatives. *LokPal must organize Agnihotra everywhere in his state, especially Janpads. Agnihotra Yagyas are done for Devi & Devatas who manage universal affairs of the state. Foolish people who have no understanding of Vedas and are usually asuric in nature oppose the position of Devis & Devatas. LokPal must immediately control such people in the state who are against the performance of Yagyas especially Agnihotra. Agnihotra Yagyas remove pollution and create goodwill in everyone's heart.*

A specialized University for women is set up to teach them values of chastity and producing good children. A stable society depends on women. Women are the basis of a happy state, they need to be educated, protected and encouraged. *Women are considered equal to men in Vedic culture. Therefore, LokPal must make specialized universities for women to enhance womanhood through education. It will ensure good progeny which will increase dharm in his state.*

A university of Vedic Values needs to be set up to ensure that Vedic literatures are properly understood. That makes the Vedic knowledge of LokPal successful. *Vedic values are universal values and they bring happiness & prosperity for all. For a stable society, education is the most important aspect. An educated society automatically promotes dharma and removes anarchy. Behavioral & Values based training creates productive citizens in the state. All education must be of the highest quality and free for all. The state taxes must pay for this system.*

100 Respecting Foreign Traders

Narada then inquires,"Whether the employees of your tax department honestly extract taxes from traders who have come to do business with traders from your country. I hope they do not tax foreign traders more than they should. Do you keep a check on your tax department employees?"

Foreign traders need to be protected as much as the domestic traders by the state. Foreign traders bring new ideas, new education and new money to the state. LokPal also needs to ensure that foreign traders don't bring any culture that goes against the culture of his state. LokPal also needs to ensure that Foreign traders don't come with an ulterior objective from an enemy. *The protection of foreign traders is directly the responsibility of LokPal. Any fraud against foreign traders must invite the strictest punishment from LokPal. No official or minister of the LokPal must tax foreign traders more than the official taxation policy of the state.*

Foreign trade should be encouraged only with friendly states. A higher tax on foreign traders from enemy states must be levied to dissuade them. If any foreign trader is promoted by an enemy state then that foreign trader must not be allowed to indulge in trade with local businesses. *Foreign traders must be charged 100% of revenues as taxes if they engage in dumping their products to destroy local industries. Any foreign trader coming with*

weapons innovation must be immediately welcome to tie up with the state of LokPal.

LokPal must provide excellent judicial services to foreign traders because Truth & Justice invites more traders to invest in the state. Foreign traders must be kept in a special zone in the state so that they are not able to mix freely with the local population. *LokPal must not only protect local businesses from unfair trade practices but also protect foreign traders from unfair trade practices. When foreign traders feel secure, then it automatically attracts more foreign investment.*

101 Ensuring Quality Imports

Narada then inquires, "Whether those foreign traders get proper goods as per your state needs and quality standards? Whether you ensure that your state employees don't cheat them?"

LokPal must create an import list, a restricted import list and also a prohibited export list to guide trade with foreign countries. LokPal must always allow balanced trade with friendly foreign nations. *LokPal must never enter into any international trade agreement involving any enemy states. Such trade pacts may force a LokPal to compromise with state security at some point in future.*

Imports should not

- Destroy local manufacturers
- Bring unwanted items
- Compete with state exports
- Be cheaper than local produce
- Sent directly to villages
- Of food

Imports should be

- Higher quality than local produce
- With the process to manufacture them
- Only introduced in cities

LokPal must ensure that state officials should not cheat foreign traders. All foreign traders must be directly protected by the state and LokPal. *LokPal must further regulate food items that may also bring diseases. LokPal must also use foreign traders to spread the values of Dharma in their countries. LokPal must also introduce training on culture and traditions for foreign traders.*

102   Learning from Experts

Narada then inquires,"Whether you keep hearing about Dharma and Artha from properly qualified and practicing experts on Dharma and Artha?"

The LokPal must regularly hear from Vedic experts. It is important for LokPal to keep reminding himself of his duties from Vedic experts. A failure to do so will put LokPal on the wrong path. At Least one hour in the morning must be spent listening to scriptures such as Mahabharata, Ramayana and Srimad Bhagavatam.

A Lokpal

- Must hear from Vedic Teachers on his responsibility
- Must be well versed in history of Mahabharat and Ramayana
- Must chant Harinam everyday
- Must treat Hari, Ram and Krishna as his only Heroes and Guides
- Must learn ArthaShastra from Vedic teachers

103   Taking care of Teachers

Narada then inquires,"Whether you regularly donate grains from your agriculture, milk and yogurt / Dahi from your cows, honey from your farms to qualified teachers for their daily dharmic activities?"

A LokPal must protect all Vedic teachers through his state machinery and officials. That is the duty of all LokPals. *LokPal must ensure that any vedic seer and priest do not lack anything. LokPal must create incentives in the state for cow & bull protection. LokPal must also encourage farmers to produce more honey through tax incentives. Bees help in preserving pollination. LokPal must also give incentive to dairies to protect older cows & bulls. After every season bulls must be left open in the fields to restore fertility in the soil. LokPal must pass a law punishable by death for those who kill cows & bulls for their flesh because these animals provide milk & yogurt throughout their living life.*

LokPal must ensure

- All Vedic teachers receive state stipend at all times
- Receive free food, medicine, milk and Dahi from state
- Encourage Sanatana Dharma activities of teachers
- Support the children of teachers of Sanatana Dharma with free education
- Sanatana Dharma teachers are protected by the State

When Vedic teachers are protected, the state becomes prosperous and auspicious. *LokPal must ensure that all dairy farms & honey farms provide free services to the residences of all great sages & seers.*

104 Technical Education

Narada then inquires, "Whether you provide all necessary raw material to your artisans and engineers of your state in an organized way, in such a quantity that those resources last at least four months of the Year. Do you ensure that this happens regularly so that there is no shortage of these at any time?"

LokPal must set up research institutions to evaluate the chemical composition of all precious stones & metals in the state. LokPal must also set up academic institutions to provide technical education on refining raw stones and metals to provide valuable metals to be used for minting and also trade. LokPal must also use these metals in building more specialized weapons to be used in the case of war. *Artisans must be promoted to ensure that their products and services are sold at high value across the world. LokPal must also encourage arts based on Vedic & Puranic stories that educate masses on the values of Dharma. LokPal must regularly buy those artifacts to decorate his offices and state buildings.*

LokPal needs to setup Universities for

- Engineers
- Artists
- Doctors
- Social reforms

LokPal needs to set up institutions for

- Mines, Metals and minerals
- Earth based raw materials
- Energy Management

- Agriculture and seed Management
- New Financial Resources
- Defense and Offense

These institutions help the state to produce experts in large quantities for future sustainability of the state. *LokPal must regularly promote education in engineering to promote science based culture in the society. The best engineers must be immediately employed in his militaries to serve the state. Weapons development creates unique civilian technologies also. LokPal must continuously modernize his weapons & ammunition to build a very strong state.*

105 Expressing Gratitude

Narada then inquires,"Whether you properly glorify a person in a large gathering, one who has performed some work for you without you even asking? When you come to know of such an act, do you personally express your gratitude to that person in private as well as in public? Do you offer that person all respect as necessary?"

A LokPal must ensure that gratitude is shown by actions as well as words. Both are equally important.

A LokPal must show his gratitude by actions through

- State stipend
- State Title

A LokPal must show his gratitude by words through

- Public glorification
- State certificate
- State benefits

The LokPal increases his popularity through these measures.

106 Summary Manuals for State Resources

Narada then inquires,"Whether you collect all summary scriptures that summarize key scriptural instructions that explain - Managing Elephants, Horses, Chariots? Whether you study them yourself and practice as per instructions?"

Instruction and Study Manuals must be created for every weapon and war equipment. A LokPal must have read or heard from those manuals At Least once. A LokPal must also witness their use at least once.

Hasti Sutra - Standard Operating Procedures for managing elephants

Ashva Sutra - Standard Operating Procedures for managing horses

Ratha Sutra - Standard Operating Procedures for managing chariots

State officials must be required by law to ensure that every single system of war is displayed in front of LokPal. Nowadays, most infantry and logistics are not based on service animals such as Elephants, Camels, Mules and Horses. This instruction of Narada can be utilized for mechanized infantry vehicles, large logistical transport planes, submarines, aircraft carriers, drones and other warfare vehicles. *Narada's instructions on maintaining Standard Operating Protocol documents are still relevant today. The entire US military ensures uniform training through simple SOP manuals.* The successful militaries use SOP to ensure uniform training as well as 'continuing leadership' program to ensure that there is a backup for every eventuality.

107 Summary Manuals for weapons

Narada then inquires,"Whether your palace has Summary Instruction manuals for Archery (Dhanurveda Sutra), Machines (Yantra Sutra) and your Population (Nagarik Sutra)? Do you regularly study them and also practice those teachings?"

Yantra Sutra: Machines that throw iron, glass, brass and stone bullets. The instruction manual for operating them is called Yantra sutra.

Nagrik Sutra: The summary instruction manuals for protecting cities and citizens is called Nagrik Sutra.

Dhanurveda Sutra: The summary instruction manuals for operating complex Bows and Arrows are called Dhanurved Sutra.

All modern weapons must be publicly displayed to the LokPal and their use must be shown to the public. Failure to do so will result in doubts on the LokPal. *Citizens must feel proud of the capability of the state to protect their interests. In the name of democracy, politicians can be easily corrupted by enemies. In such scenarios, LokPal must hide these manuals from corrupt politicians at important positions.* LokPal must regularly spy on his own advisors and secretaries to ensure that they are not corrupted by enemies behind his back. *All important original manuals must be safeguarded directly by LokPal. Generally, a LokPal is selected from a military tradition because he will then know the importance of the military in global diplomacy.*

In case of war, a SOP for citizen protection must also be maintained so that citizens are well equipped to offer resistance to the enemy. *All citizens must be trained in principles of Dhanurveda, which can be used for any modern weapon system.* Most modern weapons such as pistols as well as long range guns come into the category of Yantra Sutra. *A proper training must be given to all so that societies remain free from criminals who are often funded by enemy states. Modern democracies as well as communist states often disarm their citizens for fear of violence against the corrupt governments. However, Maharaja Yudhishthir was so capable and loved by his citizens that he empowered his citizens to gain all knowledge of different weapons that can be easily available to them. Therefore, there was no police in the governance of Yudhishthir.* Police is a colonial concept which eventually made back-roads into the colonial countries themselves. The security of the state is the joint responsibility of the state as well as its citizens. Both the state and citizens must be armed to protect Loktantra.

108   Usage of Modern Weapons

Narada then inquires,"Whether you know all types of astra (weapons that are invoked through mantra), Vedas' punishment decrees and processes, and other necessary poisons to destroy all your enemies?"

The LokPal is the ultimate decision maker of the state. He is the only one to finally declare war on the enemy. When a war is declared, LokPal must give free hand to his generals to completely destroy the enemy of the state.

The LokPal must know

- All weapon systems of the war
- All chemical and other systems of mass destruction
- Policy for each circumstance of war

The LokPal must also know

- Codes of punishment from Vedic literature
- Situations in which such codes can be applied

Enemy must know that they will be defeated in a war. That fear in the enemy ensures peace for the LokPal. *Every soldier in the army must be well informed about the goals of the war, otherwise the state loses the war. Informed & motivated soldiers are the most powerful weapon in the state's arsenal.*

LokPal must be fully aware of the capability of every weapon in his arsenal. LokPal must be aware of usage and potentiality of destruction of every weapon in his arsenal. A well informed LokPal automatically ensures victory in any battle. *Diplomacy works only when there is a credible threat of military action. Nowadays many large countries such as the United States have become powerful because they have used this principle to drive business deals and maintain their currency as a global currency.* During the time of Yudhishthir's rule, his currency 'Nishk' was the global currency. *That ensured global political control through the strength of the military and economy.*

109   Protection from Natural Calamities

Narada then inquires,"Whether you protect your state from calamities and fear arising due to fire, snakes, disease and rakshasas?"

The LokPal must ensure protection of its citizens from natural calamities as well as anti-social elements.

- Protection from floods
- Protection from fire
- Protection from wild animals
- Protection from mass epidemic diseases and contagious diseases
- Protection from Barbarians

There should be a disaster management team directly under the LokPal to take care of all of the above threats. Barbarians must be destroyed by state armies. *Modern disaster management agencies of all governments in the world nowadays do not focus on protection of all living beings. In any natural disaster, the first priority is first given to human beings which is all correct but agencies must also focus on protecting wild as well as pet animals. Rakshasas are not found today in human society because they have been forbidden to interfere in the affairs of humans by Devatas.* Barbarians are those who do not follow the principles of Dharma as given in Vedas. *Generally barbarians do not follow the rules mentioned in Vedas and they engage in unnecessary violence against innocents.* It is the responsibility of LokPal to administer tough punishment to barbarians so that they do not hurt

110   Protecting Disabled

Narada then inquires,"Whether you protect and take care of blind, muke, disabled, people born without some organs, destitute & lonely people with no relatives, and Sannyasis like a father?"

LokPal must create a separate department for the disabled. There should be medical research to ensure that the disability is minimized and root causes identified with solutions. All public places must have facilities for disabled. *All state facilities must carry special entrance and exit facilities for disabled. Ideally, a guide should be available at all state facilities to escort disabled people, if they require such help.*

When the LokPal creates these facilities, then he is loved by his citizens.

The LokPal must also

- Provide state stipend to disabled
- Reduce taxes for disabled
- Provide free education, food and medicines for disabled

Governments must always be altruistic because that creates goodwill for them. *Europeans who always say that the ancient kings were ruthless have been debunked here.* The governments which are run on the principles of Loktantra always take care of the weaker sections of society.

111 Six Vices for a LokPal

Narada then inquires, "Whether you have renounced sleep, laziness, fear, anger, Coldness of heart and procrastination? Have you left these six vices far behind?"

- Nidra - Sleep
- Alasya - Laziness
- Fear
- Anger
- Kathorta- Cruelty
- Dirghsutrata - Procrastination

Oversleeping or less sleep are both enemies of the LokPal. The LokPal must never be lazy to perform his tasks. The LokPal must be fearless in taking courageous decisions. The LokPal must be free from any anger. The LokPal must never be cruel. The LokPal must never procrastinate.

The LokPal can overcome all those faults by regularly taking shelter of Harinam which is the recommended Dharma for Kaliyug (current age) by Brahma himself.

Hare Rama Hare Rama Rama Rama Hare Hare

Hare Krishna Hare Krishna Krishna Krishna Hare Hare

Through this shelter of Harinam, LokPal becomes the source of inspiration for his citizens. LokPal has to set an example for his citizens. When LokPal derelicts his duties then the nation collapses. *Nowadays, the personal qualities of leaders are not evaluated before they are selected to run for positions. Because of which the people in democratic as well as socialistic countries are suffering.*

That's one more reason that the loktantra is better than democracy or any other political model.

112 Yudhishthira's Assurance

Yudhishthira then confirms, "Devarshi Narada, whatever instructions you have given me, I will follow them with all my heart and my sincerity. Your instructions have improved my ability to serve my state." After this King Yudhishthira followed everything that Narada Muni instructed him and attained success in ruling the entire earth including all its islands and oceans.

The LokPal gives assurance that he will follow instructions of Narada completely.

113 Narada's Satisfaction and Blessings

Narada becomes happy after Yudhishthira's pledge and announces," A Lokpal who protects all four Varnas in this way, lives very happily in this world and in the end proceeds to Indra Lok after his life"

Thus ends Narada's instructions for the LokPal. Then Yudhishthir told Narada, 'Whatever you have instructed me is very logical and Dharmic. I willingly follow your instructions. There is no doubt that in previous times, Kings have done every work with due diligence. I also want to follow in their footsteps completely, but sometimes, we are not able to do so properly.' *This shows the humility of Yudhishthir. Despite mein the most successful ruler of the world, his learning attitude shines because of his humility. Contrast this to politicians of current times, who often ignore wise lessons from history in the name of practicality assuming that they know better today. The instructions of Narada Muni to Yudhishthir are conclusive, because they cover all aspects of effective governance.*

Narada Muni instructs on:

1. *Personal qualities of Lokpal or a leader*
2. *Policies towards economic growth*
3. *Defense Policy*
4. *Personal Protection of leader*
5. *Selecting Cabinet*
6. *Offensive & Defensive warfare*
7. *Restoring Dharma in the society*

Thus completes the rendering of Narada Muni's instructions to Yudhishthir on 'How to become a Statesman?'

Pledge & Score for the Statesman

As a LokPal or Statesman, I scored _____ out of 111 points.

I take a vow to rule my subjects as per the instructions that I have read and understood.

Signed:

Name:

Place:

Date & Time:

About Author

Aditya Satsangi has been a lifelong student of Vyasadeva's literary compositions such as Mahabharata and Bhagavad Purana. His fascination in Vedas started with his Maternal Grandmother, Srimati Brahma Devi, who taught him the glories of an Ancient King, Prahlad who went on to become one of the most successful kings of the world.

Later Prabhupada's translations inspired him to study works of Sri Ramanuja (Vishishtadvaita), Adi Shankara (Advaita), MadhvaCharya (Dvaita) and Teachings of Chaitanya Mahaprabhu.

This book is a humble attempt to bring forth a small section of work of Mahabharata of the original author Sri Vyasadeva in English language. Author hopes that politicians and students of Politics will use this book for the benefit of the people they govern.

Good Politics helps everyone. Therefore politicians play a very important role in society. The ancient histories mentioned in Vedic literatures speak of a much more sophisticated political system prevalent in society that helped a much larger population.

The modern institution of governance is based on historical experiences of the last 500 years. However, we all know that our civilization is much older than the last 500 years and more successful political systems have existed in the past.

From history we know that Chanakya guided Chandra Gupta to victory using the Principles of good politics as taught by Narada Muni to Yudhishthira, Dhruv and Prahlad. In this book, it is my humble attempt to bring forth authentic versions from Vedic Shastra and Purana.

Notes & References

> Mahabharat by Vyasadeva (Published by Gita Press, Gorakhpur)

➤ Srimad Bhagavatam

➤ Srila Prabhupada's conversations

➤ Madhvacharya Commentaries

Definitions

1. Kartavya - duties born out of responsibility
2. Karma - Past Actions whose results haven't fructified, past actions whose results have fructified, past actions whose results you are living today
3. Dharma - compulsory duty
4. Humility - to not be anxious for the satisfaction of being honored by others (Prabhupada)
5. Artha Shastra - Science of Economic, Social wellbeing for the society
6. Shastra - Vedic Literatures
7. Vedas - Original body of knowledge. Word of Vishnu
8. Shruti: Unchangeable aspect of Vedic Literatures
9. Smriti: Can be modified as per the time, place and circumstance. But must follow Shruti in spirit
10. Hari: A common name of God
11. Krishna: The name of Supreme Personality of Godhead
12. Vedanta: Summary study of Veda
13. Vyasadeva: The Literary Incarnation of Vishnu and author of Mahabharata; compiler of all Vedas
14. Godhead: Krishna
15. Vasudeva: Another name of Krishna
16. Pradyumna: Another incarnation of Krishna
17. Aniruddha: Another incarnation of Krishna
18. Sankarshana: Another incarnation of Krishna
19. Godhead: same as 14
20. Vishnu: God's another name; Controller of mode of Goodness
21. Yudhishthir: Son of Pandu and Emperor of world
22. Dharma: same as 3
23. Muni: Thinker and Scientist
24. Bhagavan: Possessor of six opulences - All Beauty, All Knowledge, All Wealth, All Strength, All Happiness and All Renunciation
25. Varnashrama: A system of four Varna and Four Ashrama
26. Varna: Category
27. Brahmin: Teacher
28. Vaishya: Trader, Agriculturist and Cow Protector

29. Shudra: Once who does service to others on payment
30. Artha: Economics
31. Maharaja: A King
32. Vedic: Conforming to Vedas
33. Mantrana:: Professional Advice
34. Arthashastra: A Vedic system of Economy, Governance and Trade
35. Mahabharata: History of Greater India; Instructions with deep meaning
36. Deva: a Controlling deity representing God
37. Daiva: of Deva
38. Manush: of Humans
39. Lekhak: Writer
40. Ganak: Accountant
41. Panchayat: A system of governance by five important and qualified people in a village
42. Raj: Government
43. Yamaraja: Supervises death of all living entities
44. Dharmaraj: Absolute authority on Dharma
45. Bhupal: A small ruler of land , works under LokPal
46. Ramayana: History of Ram, written by Valmiki
47. Bhaktivedanta: A title given to a person who is a Guru in Bhakti tradition
48. Bharat: Ancient Name of Asia with capital in India
49. Mandarachal: a Divine mountain
50. Vedantist: Follower of Vedanta Sutra, a summary of Veda

Bibliography

➤ Maharabharat (Sanskrit-Hindi) Original of Vyasadeva printed by Gita Press, Gorakhpur

➤ Lectures and Conversations by many prominent historians many other saints on YouTube from different traditions

Other Books by Author

➤ Samrat Yudhishthir - The Greatest Emperor
➤ Karma is a B*tch
➤ The Gita
➤ The Hindu Bible

➤ Sattology - Debunking Mythology
➤ Pandavas - The Famous Five
➤ One Arrow, One Kill
➤ Gold, Glory & God - A curse on the natives
➤ Transcending the Mind - Yog Sutra As It Is

Made in the USA
Columbia, SC
01 December 2022

72321708R00186